Grace
& Truth

Grace
& Truth
A Holy Pursuit

Oswald Chambers

Compiled and Edited by
JULIE ACKERMAN LINK

DISCOVERY HOUSE
PUBLISHERS

Grace & Truth: A Holy Pursuit
© 2013 by Oswald Chambers Publications Association
Limited. All rights reserved.

Discovery House Publishers is affiliated with RBC
Ministries, Grand Rapids, Michigan.

All Scripture quotations, unless otherwise indicated,
are from the New King James Version. Copyright ©
1979, 1980, 1982 by Thomas Nelson, Inc., Publishers.

Questions by Julie Ackerman Link

ISBN: 978-1-57293-793-2

Printed in the United States of America

First printing in 2013

Contents

Introduction

> For the law was given through Moses, but grace
> and truth came through Jesus Christ. (John 1:17)

GRACE AND TRUTH are difficult to reconcile. The two
concepts seem contradictory. Truth seems harsh; grace
seems soft. Truth seems rigid; grace seems flexible. Grace
seems like an exception to truth. The way of grace seems
like a detour around truth. With such a strong demand
for truth in Scripture, where can we find room for grace?
Oswald Chambers helps us to see that the two really are
compatible.

According to Chambers, grace is "the overflowing
nature of God." As evidence, he points to creation. When
we observe nature, he says, "we have no words to describe
the lavishness of God." Nature proves that God is gracious
to everyone—not to an elite few.

And truth, says Chambers, means more than accuracy.
It means "accuracy about something that corresponds with
God."

Using these and other statements, Chambers shows
that grace is not an exception to truth but a holy expression
of truth. Grace is true because it accurately describes God's

interaction with us. Therefore grace is a true expression of God's character. And truth is grace because it applies to all and is available to everyone.

Instead of being archrivals, grace and truth are intimate companions. They travel together wooing and winning people to live in the safe shelter of a loving heavenly Father.

Although the concepts seem worlds apart in today's way of thinking, we have the assurance that they are not. In Christ, grace and truth are reconciled, which means that we can be both gracious and truthful.

> The Word became flesh and made his dwelling among us. We have seen his glory, the glory of the one and only Son, who came from the Father, full of grace and truth. (John 1:14 NIV)

Grace

God's Overflowing Favor

⏎NCEPTION WHICH Jesus Christ had of society was that men might be one with Him as He was one with the Father. There is a difference between being saved and sanctified by the sheer sovereign grace of God and choosing to be the choice ones, not for heaven, but down here. The average view of Christianity, that we only need to have faith and we are saved, is a stumbling block. How many of us care anything about being witnesses to Jesus Christ? How many of us are willing to spend every ounce of energy we have, every bit of mental, moral and spiritual life for Jesus Christ? That is the meaning of a worker in God's sense.[AUG]

Reflection Questions
Have I been lounging in the life of faith
or working with God to bring citizens
into His kingdom?

MANY DELIBERATELY CHOOSE to be workers for God, but they have no matter of God's mighty grace in them, no matter from God's mighty word. The pattern for God's worker is that he is entrusted with a mission. We have to be in God's hand because we are being made co-workers with God.[AUG]

Grace: God's Overflowing Favor

A WORKER FOR God must be prepared to endure hardness, to soak up all the bad and turn it into good, and nothing but the supernatural grace of God and his sense of obligation will enable him to do it. We will be brought into relationship with people for whom we have no affinity. The one mastering obligation of our life is to persuade men for Jesus Christ. To do that we have to learn to live among the fact of human stuff as it is, not as it ought to be; and the fact of Bible revelation, whether it agrees with our doctrines or not.[AUG]

Reflection Questions

Am I allowing God's standard to obsess me?

Am I measuring my life by His at all times?

JESUS CHRIST'S STANDARD for us is Himself. We have to be saturated in this ideal in thinking and in praying, and allow nothing to blur the standard. We must lift up Jesus Christ not only in the preaching of the Gospel but to our own souls. If my mind and heart and spirit is getting fixed with one Figure only, the Lord Jesus Christ, and other people and other ideas are fading, then I am growing in grace.[AUG]

FORGIVENESS IS THE Divine miracle of grace. Have we ever contemplated the amazing fact that God through the Death of Jesus Christ forgives us for every wrong we have ever done, not because we are sorry, but out of His sheer mercy? God's forgiveness is only natural in the supernatural domain. Being born again of the Spirit is an unmistakable work of God, as mysterious as the wind. Beware of the tendency to water down the supernatural in religion.ᴬᵁᴳ

Reflection Questions

In what ways have I minimized the work of grace in my life? Am I generous or stingy with God's grace?

NEVER SAY GOD'S holiness does not mean what it does mean. It means every part of the life under the scrutiny of God, knowing that the grace of God is sufficient for every detail. The temptation comes along the line of compromise. Never tolerate by sympathy with yourself or with others any practice that is not in keeping with a holy God.ᴬᵁᴳ

Grace: God's Overflowing Favor

THERE IS A difference between devotion to principles and devotion to a person. Hundreds of people today are devoting themselves to phases of truth, to causes. Jesus Christ never asks us to devote ourselves to a cause or a creed; He asks us to devote ourselves to Him, to sign away the right to ourselves and yield to Him absolutely, and take up that cross daily. The cross Jesus asks us to take up cannot be suffering for conviction's sake, because a man will suffer for conviction's sake whether he is a Christian or not. Neither can it be suffering for conscience' sake, because a man will go to martyrdom for his principles without having one spark of the grace of God in his heart.[AUG]

Reflection Questions

Am I devoted to a principle or to a person?
Has the spark of God's grace ignited a fire of devotion or barely a flicker of faith?

THE GRACE WE had yesterday won't do for today. "The grace of God"—the overflowing favor of God; we can always reckon it is there to draw on if we don't trust our own merits (see 2 Corinthians 5:18–21).[AUG]

ARE THOSE OF us who have experienced God's regenerating grace prepared to go the whole length with Jesus Christ? Are we prepared to let the Holy Spirit search us until we know what the disposition of sin is, the thing that rules and works its own way, that lusts against the Spirit of God that is in us? Will we agree with God's verdict that that disposition should be identified with the death of Jesus? If so, then thank God, it will be as dead in us as the dead Christ was as a crucified body. Beware of going on the line of—I am reckoning myself to be "dead indeed unto sin"—unless you have been through the radical issue of will with God. ᴬᵁᴳ

Reflection Questions

How far have I gone with Jesus? Am I willing to be identified with His death to the extent that every enemy of grace within me will be crucified with Him?

IF WE GIVE ourselves over to God, there is no end to our development and growth in grace. Our Lord has no fear of the consequences when once the heart is open toward Him.ᴮᴾ

Grace: *God's Overflowing Favor*

Sɪɴ ɪs ɴᴏᴛ man's problem, but God's. God has taken the problem of sin into His own hands and solved it, and the proof that He has is the Cross of Calvary. Pseudo-evangelism has twisted the revelation and made it mean—"Now that God has saved me, I do not need to do anything." The New Testament revelation is that now I am saved by God's grace, I must work on that basis and keep myself clean. It does not matter what a man's heredity is, or what tendencies there are in him, on the basis of the Redemption he can become all that God's Book indicates he should be.ᴮꜰᴮ

Reflection Questions

In what ways do I try to solve the problem of sin on my own? How does the grace of God keep my heart and mind pure and blameless?

Tʜᴇʀᴇ ɪs ᴀɴ idea abroad today that because as Christians we are not under law, but under grace, therefore the Ten Commandments have no meaning for us— what did Jesus say? He demands that we have such a condition of heart that we never even think of doing them, every thought and imagination of heart and mind is to be unblameable in the sight of God.ᴮᴇ

WHEN WE ARE young in grace there is a note of independence about our spiritual life. It is an independence based on inexperience, an immature fellowship; it lacks the essential of devotion. Some of us remain true to the independent following and never get beyond it; but we are built for God, Himself, not for service for God.^{AUG}

Reflection Questions

How am I maturing in grace? Am I willing to dispense grace without stinginess? Am I willing to give up my independence to become part of a community of believers who give unreservedly from the treasure that God has entrusted to us?

AS WE DRAW on the grace of God He increases voluntary poverty all along the line. Always give the best you have got every time; never think about who you are giving it to, let other people take it or leave it as they choose. Pour out the best you have, and always be poor. Never reserve anything, never be diplomatic and careful about the treasure God gives.^{AUG}

Grace: *God's Overflowing Favor*

IF WE KEEP practicing, what we practice becomes our second nature, then in a crisis and in the details of life we shall find that not only will the grace of God stand by us, but also our own nature. Whereas if we refuse to practice, it is not God's grace but our own nature that fails when the crisis comes, because we have not been practicing in actual life. We may ask God to help us but He cannot, unless we have made our nature our ally.^AUG

Reflection Questions

In what situations have I practiced God's grace? In what situations have I failed to practice God's grace? Am I walking in the integrity of God's testimony of grace?

YOU CANNOT DRAW on the grace of God for testimony if these three things are not there—the word of God, the power of God, and the consciousness that you are walking in the integrity of that testimony in private.^AUG

OUR PRIVATE LIFE is disciplined by the interference of people in our own matters. People who do not mean to be a trial are a trial. That is where the test for patience comes. Have we failed the grace of God there? It is not feeling the grace of God, it is drawing on it now. Whatever is our particular condition we are sure to have one of these things Paul mentions—afflictions, necessities, distresses. It is not praying to God and asking Him to help us in these things, it is taking the grace of God now. Many of us make prayer the preparation for work, it is never that in the Bible.^AUG

Reflection Questions

Am I able to be gracious to people who annoy me, insult me, and hurt me? If the place where God has put me is a laboratory to examine my life for evidence of grace, what will He find?

GOD PUTS HIS saints into places where they have to exhibit long-suffering. Let circumstances pull and don't give way to any intemperance whatever, but in all these things draw on the grace of God and He will make you a marvel to yourself and to others.^AUGv

Grace: God's Overflowing Favor

WE ARE ALWAYS inclined to be intemperate about our religion, it is the last thing for which we learn to draw on the grace of God. In our praying we draw on our memories, on our past experiences, on our present desires. We only learn to draw on the grace of God by pureness, by knowledge, by long-suffering. We want to get short cuts to knowledge and because we cannot take them we rush off into intemperate work. The craze in everyone's blood nowadays is a disease of external activities.[AUG]

Reflection Questions

Have I substituted activity for devotion? Have I mistaken information for wisdom? Have I paid more attention to the promise of greatness than to the call to humility?

ONE OF THE greatest proofs that we are drawing on the grace of God is that we can be humiliated without the slightest trace of anything but the grace of God in us. Draw on the grace of God now, not presently. The one word in the spiritual vocabulary is "NOW."[AUG]

WE HAVE TO recognize that we are one half mechanical and one half mysterious; to live in either domain and ignore the other is to be a fool or a fanatic. The great supernatural work of God's grace is in the incalculable part of our nature; we have to work out in the mechanical realm what God works in in the mysterious realm. People accept creeds, but they will not accept the holy standards of Jesus Christ's teaching. To build on the fundamental work of God's grace and ignore the fact that we have to work it out in a mechanical life produces those who divorce the mysterious life and the practical life, but the mysterious and the mechanical are welded together (John 13).[BE]

Reflection Questions

Is my life of faith more mechanical or mystical? Why? In what ways is God's supernatural work of grace in me being worked out on behalf of those who are strangers to grace?

JESUS CHRIST TEACHES that if we have had a work of grace done in our hearts, we will show to our fellow-men the same love God has shown to us.[BP]

Grace: God's Overflowing Favor

CHRISTIANITY TAKES ALL the emotions, all the dangerous elements of human nature, the things which lead us astray, all feelings and excitabilities, and makes them into one great power for God. Other religions either cut out dangerous emotions altogether or base too much on them. The tendency is to say, "You must not trust in feelings"; perfectly true, but if your religion is without feeling, there is nothing in it. If you are living a life right with God, you will have feeling, most emphatically so, but you will never run the risk of basing your faith on feelings. The Christian is one who bases his whole confidence in God and His work of grace, then the emotions become the beautiful ornament of the life, not the source of it.[BE]

Reflection Questions

In what ways has grace brought my thoughts and feelings into balance? What still needs to be accomplished?

GOD PUTS THE law of grace where the law of nature works, that is, in the heart. Thank God for His sovereign grace which can alter the mainspring of life![BP]

IF WE DO not fit ourselves by practice when there is no crisis, we shall find that our nature will fail us when the crisis comes. The grace of God never fails, but we may fail the grace of God. When your nervous system, which has been ruled by the wrong disposition, is inclined to say "I can't," you must say, "You must," and to your amazement you find you can!BE

Reflection Questions

In what situations have I failed the grace of God? What circumstances tempt me to place my trust in rules rather than follow the Spirit in the way of grace?

WE SHALL COME to find that being "not under the law, but under grace" does not mean we are so free from the law that it does not matter now what we do; it means that in our actual lives we can fulfil all the requirements of the law of God.BE

Grace: God's Overflowing Favor

THE DANGER OF certain religious movements is that the emphasis is put not on the regenerating power of the grace of God, but on individual consecration, individual fasting and prayer, individual devotion to God. The apostle Paul sums up individual human effort under the guise of religion as things which have "a shew of wisdom in will, worship, and humility, and neglecting of the body" (Colossians 2:23). It is simply individualism veneered over with religious phraseology.[BE]

Reflection Questions

Do I rely on my own effort or on God's grace?
Do I cover what I cannot change or do I allow God to clean up all my religious polish?

JESUS CHRIST DID not come to tell us to be holy, but to make us holy, undeserving of censure in the sight of God. If any man or woman gets there it is by the sheer supernatural grace of God. You can't indulge in pious pretence when you come to the atmosphere of the Bible. If there is one thing the Spirit of God does it is to purge us from all sanctimonious humbug, there is no room for it.[BE]

HABITS ARE BUILT up, not by theory, but by practice. The one great problem in spiritual life is whether we are going to put God's grace into practice. God won't do the mechanical; He created us to do that; but we can only do it while we draw on the mysterious realm of His Divine grace. Whenever in devotion before God His Spirit gives a clear indication of what He wants you to do, do it.[BE]

Reflection Questions

In what ways do I practice grace? Do I respond quickly to the prompting of the Holy Spirit or do I ask for a second opinion?

SPIRITUAL EDUCATION AND habit go together in this connection: I learn to make my body act quickly along the line of education the Holy Spirit has given me, then when I find myself in new circumstances I shall not be helpless because I have educated myself according to the laws of God's grace.[BE]

Grace: *God's Overflowing Favor*

EMOTIONS IN NATURE and in grace need a strong controlling power. In natural life people who have successive emotions are in danger of becoming sentimentalists; in spiritual life successive emotions lead to being driven about by every wind of doctrine. In spiritual life successive emotions are more dangerous. If you are without the control of the Spirit of God, devotional emotion and religious excitement always end in sensuality. Emotions that stir feelings must act themselves out, whether rightly or wrongly will depend on the person.[BE]

Reflection Questions

Do I allow my emotions more control than they deserve? How can I discern between feelings based on my own sympathies and those prompted by God's grace?

WE MUST BRING our bodily life into line by practice moment by moment. Then when the crisis comes we shall find not only God's grace but our own nature will stand by us, and the crisis will pass without any disaster at all, but exactly the opposite will happen, the soul will be built up into a stronger attitude toward God.[BP]

IF YOU OBEY the Spirit of God and practice in your physical life all that God has put in your heart by His Spirit, when the crisis comes you will find your nature will stand by you. So many people misunderstand why they fall. It comes from this idea, "Now I have received the grace of God, I am all right." If we do not go on practicing day by day and week by week, working out what God has worked in, when a crisis comes God's grace is there right enough, but our nature is not. Our nature has not been brought into line by practice and consequently does not stand by us, and down we go and then we blame God.[BP]

Reflection Questions
In what circumstances do I blame God
for my own failure? Why?

WHEN YOU STAND on the platform of God's grace, you see instantly the bondage that is in the world. The etiquette and standards of the world are an absolute bondage, and those who live in them are abject slaves, and yet the extraordinary thing is that when a worldly person sees anyone emancipated and under the yoke of the Lord Jesus Christ, he says they are in bondage, whereas exactly the opposite is true.[BP]

Grace: God's Overflowing Favor

To "ESTIMATE" MEANS to reckon the value. Estimates are made in the heart, and God alters our estimates. Those of you who have received God's Spirit and know His grace experimentally, watch how He has altered your estimate of things. It used to matter a lot what your worldly crowd thought about you: how much does it matter now? You used to estimate highly the good opinion of certain people: how do you estimate it now? You used to estimate that immoral conduct was the worst crime on earth, but how do you estimate it now? We are horrified at immoral conduct in social life, but how many of us are as horrified at pride as Jesus Christ was?[BP]

Reflection Questions

*How has grace changed my way of thinking?
What do I try to do for God that
only He can do?*

BEWARE OF TRYING to do what God alone can do, and of blaming God for not doing what we alone can do. We try to save ourselves, but God only can do that. We try to sanctify ourselves, but God only can do that. After God has done these sovereign works of grace in our hearts, we have to work them out in our lives.[BP]

GOD LOVES THE world so much that He goes all lengths to remove the wrong from it, and we must have the same kind of love. Any other kind of love for the world simply means that we take it as it is and are perfectly delighted with it. It is that sentiment which is the enemy of God. Do we love the world sufficiently to spend and be spent so that God can manifest His grace through us until the wrong and the evil are removed?[BP]

Reflection Questions

In what ways do I manifest grace on God's behalf? Am I more likely to stand up for God or for my own reputation? What makes me afraid of the lies that Satan tells about me?

OUR ESTIMATE OF honor measures our growth in grace. What we stand up for proves what our character is like. If we stand up for our reputation it is a sign it needs standing up for! God never stands up for His saints, they do not need it. The devil tells lies about men, but no slander on earth can alter a man's character.[BP]

Grace: _God's Overflowing Favor_

THE NATURAL HEART does not want the Gospel. We will take God's blessings and His loving-kindnesses and prosperity, but when God's Spirit informs us that we have to give up the rule of ourselves and let Him rule us, then we understand what Paul means when he says the "carnal mind is enmity against God." The wonderful work of the grace of God is that through the Atonement God can alter the center of my life, and put there a supreme, passionate devotion to God Himself.[BP]

Reflection Questions

Why do I resist grace? What am I holding onto that could be any better than what God wants to give me?

WHEREVER THE GRACE of God works effectually in a man's inner nature, his nervous system is altered and the external world begins to take on a new guise. Why? Because he has a new disposition, he is a "new creature," and he will begin to see things differently.[BP]

THE ESSENCE OF the Gospel of God working through conscience and conduct is that it shows itself at once in action. God can make simple, guileless people out of cunning, crafty people; that is the marvel of the grace of God. It can take the strands of evil and twistedness out of a man's mind and imagination and make him simple toward God, so that his life becomes radiantly beautiful by the miracle of God's grace.[BP]

Reflection Questions

In what ways am I different because of God's grace? Am I willing to be simply good rather than devilishly complex? Do I avoid strangers or willingly and happily entertain them?

HAVE YOU EVER noticed how God's grace comes to His children who are given to hospitality? Prosperity in home, in business, and in every way comes from following God's instructions in each detail.[BP]

Grace: God's Overflowing Favor

SPIRITUAL MATURITY IS not reached by the passing of the years, but by obedience to the will of God. Some people mature into an understanding of God's will more quickly than others because they obey more readily, they more readily sacrifice the life of nature to the will of God, they more easily swing clear of little determined opinions. It is these little determined opinions, convictions of our own that won't budge, that hinder growth in grace and make us bitter and dogmatic, intolerant, and utterly un-Christlike.[BSUG]

Reflection Questions

Do I wonder why others seem closer to God than I am? Do I notice that others more easily give up harmful habits? Do I hold on to harsh opinions and intolerant attitudes? What makes them so important to me?

JESUS "ADVANCED IN wisdom" by applying His will to the will of His Father. "For Christ also pleased not Himself." To do what we like always ends in immorality; to do what God would have us do always ends in growth in grace.[BSUG]

THERE ARE STAGES in spiritual development when God allows us to be dull, times when we cannot realize or feel anything. It is one of the greatest mercies that we have those blank spaces, for if we go on with spiritual perception too quickly we have no time to work it out; and if we have no time to work it out it will react in stagnation and degeneration. Unless religious emotions spring from the indwelling grace of God and are worked out on the right level, they will always, not sometimes, react on an immoral level.[BSUG]

Reflection Questions

In what ways have I been blessed by the blank spaces in my spiritual development? In what ways have I been tempted to "fill in" the blank spaces? What has God accomplished when I thought He was doing nothing?

THE SENSE OF utter impoverishment spiritually is a blessed pain because it is pain that takes us to God and His gracious rule and kingdom. "Blessed are the poor in spirit: for theirs is the kingdom of heaven."[CD]

Grace: *God's Overflowing Favor*

FACE FACTS. VERY few of us will face facts, we prefer our fictions. Our Lord teaches us to look things full in the face and He says: 'When you hear of wars and disturbances, do not be scared.' It is the most natural thing in the world to be scared. There is no natural heart of man or woman that is not scared by these things, and the evidence that God's grace is at work among us is that we do not get terrified.[CD]

Reflection Questions

What facts am I afraid of? How does God's grace keep me calm? What problem am I facing that reveals my lack of trust in God's grace?

IT IS VERY easy to trust in God when there is no difficulty, but that is not trust at all, it is simply letting the mind rest in a complacent mood; but when there is sickness in the house, when there is trouble, when there is death, where is our trust in God? The clearest evidence that God's grace is at work in our hearts is that we do not get into panics.[CD]

THE MAN WHO reforms without any knowledge of the grace of God is the subtlest infidel with regard to the need of regeneration. It is a good thing to have the heart swept, but it becomes the worst thing if the heart is left vacant for spirits more evil than itself to enter. Jesus said that "the last state of that man becometh worse than the first." Reformation is a good thing, but like every other good thing it is the enemy of the best. Regeneration means filling the heart with the Holy Spirit.ᶜᴴᴵ

Reflection Questions

Does the grace of God fill my heart or have I swept it clean and left it empty? Am I willing to receive grace from God or is grace too messy?

WHEN WE ASK "grace before meal" let us remember that it is not to be a mere pious custom, but a real reception of the idea of Jesus that God enables us to receive our daily bread from Him. I sometimes wonder if there would be as much chronic indigestion as there is if we received our ideas from God as Jesus would have us do.ᶜᴰ

Grace: *God's Overflowing Favor*

IT IS QUITE possible to have an intellectual appreciation of the Redemption without any experience of supernatural grace; an experience of supernatural grace comes by committing myself to a person, not to a creed or a conviction. I can never find Reality by looking within; the only way I can get at Reality is by dumping myself outside myself on to Someone else, that is, God.[CHI]

Reflection Questions

Is grace a powerful reality in my life or merely a consoling idea? Has the supernatural grace of God brought me to a place of sorrow for the wrong I have done? Does grace change my behavior or simply soothe my mind?

WE ALL EXPERIENCE remorse, disgust with ourselves over the wrong we have done when we are found out by it, but the rarest miracle of God's grace is the sorrow that puts an end for ever to the thing for which I am sorry. Repentance involves the receiving of a totally new disposition so that I never do the wrong thing again.[CHI]

I DON'T KNOW what your natural heart was like before God saved you, but I know what mine was like. I was misunderstood and misrepresented; everybody else was wrong and I was right. Then when God came and gave me a spring-cleaning, dealt with my sin, and filled me with the Holy Spirit, I began to find an extraordinary alteration in myself. The great marvel of the experience of salvation is not the alteration others see in you, but the alteration you find in yourself. When you come across certain people and things and remember what you used to be like in connection with them, and realize what you are now by the grace of God, you are filled with astonishment and joy; where there used to be a well of resentment and bitterness, there is now a well of sweetness.[CHI]

Reflection Questions

Am I only able to see the wrong that others do or am I willing to have others tell me where I am wrong? Do I respond with sweetness or bitterness when confronted with my own faults?

I AM NEVER dismayed at what I discover in myself, but learn to trust only what the grace of God does in me.[CHI]

Grace: God's Overflowing Favor

HOLINESS IS THE only sign that a man is repentant in the New Testament sense, and a holy man is not one who has his eyes set on his own whiteness, but one who is personally and passionately devoted to the Lord who saved him—one whom the Holy Ghost takes care shall never forget that God has made him what he is by sheer sovereign grace. Accept as the tender touch of God, not as a snare of the devil, every memory of sin the Holy Ghost brings home to you, keeping you in the place where you remember what you once were and what you now are by His grace.[CHI]

Reflection Questions

Why do I so quickly forget where I would be without grace? What makes me think I have the right to deny grace to someone else?

MAY THE CONVICTION of God come with swift and stern rebuke upon any one who is remembering the past of another, and deliberately choosing to forget their restoration through God's grace. When a servant of God meets these sins in others, let him be reverent with what he does not understand and leave God to deal with them.[CHI]

IF EXCELLENCE OF character is made the test, the grace of God is "made void," because a man can develop an amazing perfection of character without a spark of the grace of God. If we put a saint or a good man as the standard, we blind ourselves to ourselves, personal vanity makes us do it; there is no room for personal vanity when the standard is seen to be God Himself.[DI]

Reflection Questions

How much do I rely on my own "excellent" character? How does this make me a backslider rather than a saint? How often do I reach out to those who don't yet know God's grace?

SHOW SUCH A servant of God the backslider, the sinner steeped in the iniquity of our cities, and there will spring up in his heart an amazing well of compassion and love for that one, because he has himself experienced the grace of God which goes to the uttermost depths of sin and lifts to the highest heights of salvation.[CHI]

Grace: God's Overflowing Favor

WE HAVE TO distinguish between acquiring and receiving. We acquire habits of prayer and Bible reading and we receive our salvation, we receive the Holy Spirit, we receive the grace of God. We give more attention to the things we acquire; God pays attention to what we receive. Those things we receive can never be taken from us because God holds those who receive His gifts.[DI]

Reflection Questions

Why do I value things that I acquire by my own effort more than those I receive by God's grace? Why is it so difficult to see and appreciate the difference? How can I become more grateful for what I receive through no effort of my own?

GOD DOES NOT ask us to be good men and women; He asks us to understand that we are not good; to believe that "none is good, save one, even God," and that the grace of God was manifested in the Redemption that it might cover the incompleteness of man.[DI]

THE BIBLE IS not a book containing communications from God, it is God's revelation of Himself, in the interests of grace; God's giving of Himself in the limitation of words. The Bible is not a romance to beguile us for a while from the sordid realities of life, it is the Divine complement of the laws of Nature, of Conscience and of Humanity. It introduces us to a new universe of revelation facts not known to unregenerate commonsense.ᴳᵂ

Reflection Questions

Why is my concept of grace limited to what God does for me? Why can I not see the wonders of common grace given to all through the marvels of creation and the laws of the universe?

GOD'S BLESSINGS FALL, like His rain, on evil and good alike. The great blessings of health, genius, prosperity, all come from His overflowing grace, and not from the condition of the character of the recipients. If health were a sign that a man is right with God, we should lose all distinction as to what a good character is, for many bad men enjoy good health.ᴳᵂ

Grace: *God's Overflowing Favor*

GOD'S HOLY NAME is profaned when we put before people what God's grace has wrought in us instead of God Himself. Whenever we go into work for God from any standpoint saving that of the dominance of God, we begin to patronize at once. Unless we go as the bond-servants of Jesus Christ we have no business to go at all. Never deal with people from the superior person's standpoint. God never blesses that. Deal only by steadily presenting the Lord Jesus Christ. The characteristic of the holiness which is the outcome of the indwelling of God is a blazing truthfulness with regard to God's word, and an amazing tenderness in personal dealing.GW

Reflection Questions

In what ways have I profaned God's name by focusing on myself rather than God? In what ways do I treat God more like a sympathetic listener than a sovereign Savior?

JESUS CHRIST IS not a mere sympathizer, He is a Savior, and the only One. The sympathy is merely the accompaniment of the deliverance wrought by coming to the throne of grace and finding help in time of need.GW

THE EFFECT OF being justified by God's grace is that He begins to entrust us with the realization of what sin is. It is the saint who knows what sin is; it is the man who has been identified with the death of Jesus who begins to get the first inkling of what sin is, because the only Being who knows what sin is, is not the sinner, but God. The only One who knows what the elemental human heart is like, is not the sinner, but Jesus Christ.ᴳᵂ

Reflection Questions

Has God entrusted me with the realization of what sin is? How has it changed my attitude toward myself and other sinners? How has it changed my attitude about my own virtue?

PURITY IN GOD'S children is not the outcome of obedience to His law, but the result of the supernatural work of His grace. In the absolute humility that is produced there is never any fear of spiritual pride, never any fear of forgetting that God sends us into work for His own glory; never any fear of being harsh or unjust to others, because God has shown us what we were, and we have realized it with shame.ᴳᵂ

Grace: God's Overflowing Favor

SATAN IS NOT partially overcome; he is absolutely overcome. Every bit of his armor wherein he trusted is taken from him. The presence of Jesus means the total expulsion of Satan. When we are born again the Holy Spirit brings to us the realization of what Jesus Christ has done, and the great emancipating point of personal experience is not that we have power to overcome, but that He has overcome; then the Holy Spirit instructs us all along the line how we can successfully battle against the encroachments of Satan. When by God's grace we enter into the amazing liberty of salvation and sanctification, then comes the responsibility of walking in the light, and as we keep in the light we are able to identify ourselves with Jesus Christ's victory in such a way that it is manifested in us.GW

Reflection Questions

Have I entered the liberty of God's full and final victory over Satan and sin? Or do I live as if God's grace has more to accomplish?

THERE IS NO condescension in grace. A sinner is never afraid of Jesus.HSGM

NEVER HAVE THE idea that you are going to persuade men to believe in God. The thing that staggers the worker is that men will not believe. How can they believe, when every spring of life is impure? The great need is to have a channel through which the grace of God can come to them and do something in their unconscious life. Then slowly as that breaks into the conscious life there will come an expression of belief, because they see Jesus; but the way they see Him is through the worker who is a sacramental personality.ᴳᵂ

Reflection Questions

Where do I see the most visible evidence of God's grace at work? How is God using grace to reconcile friends and family to Himself? Am I a help or a hindrance to the work of grace? How can I be a better helper?

YOU CANNOT ARGUE men into coming to Jesus, or socialize them into coming. Only one thing will do it, and that is the power of the Gospel drawing men by the constraint of God's grace.ᴳᵂ

Grace: God's Overflowing Favor

WHEN FIRST WE experience the grace of God, we have the feeling that if ever we should become what Jesus Christ wants us to be, He would have to take us straight to Heaven! But then we discover that the place where grace takes us is not a perilous mountain peak but a broad plateau, with any amount of room to walk, as safe and as eternal as the hills. Everywhere your foot treads, at home or abroad, should bring a preparation of the gospel of peace.ᴳᵂ

Reflection Questions

Where has the grace of God taken me? Where is it leading me? Is my attitude toward sinners the same as that of Jesus? Am I preparing the way for His gospel of peace?

OUR LORD NEVER talked in stages of experience, that is, He does not talk to our heads, He instructs us in our relationship to Himself. Jesus deals with the grace of God toward sinners, and the characteristic of the grace of God is that it wells up into everlasting life, "a fountain of living water"—not merely a clean heart, but a full one, being kept clean.ᴴˢᴳᴹ

INTELLECT IS NEVER first in spiritual life. We are not born again by thinking about it, we are born again by the power of God. Intellect comes second both in nature and in grace. The things we can express intellectually are the things that are old in our experience; the things that are recent and make us what we are, we cannot define. People say, "You must believe certain things before you can be a Christian." It is impossible. A man's beliefs are the effect of his being a Christian, not the cause of it.[HSGM]

Reflection Questions

Do I give intellect a more prominent place than God gives it? Do I have higher standards of belief than God has? Do I give grace its proper place or do I make it subservient to intelligence?

HOW CAN I have the nature of Jesus? By being born from above, by the Holy Spirit coming into me on the ground of the Redemption and putting into me the disposition of Jesus. It is all done by the miracle of God's grace.[HSGM]

46

Grace: God's Overflowing Favor

THE MOST MARVELOUS ingredient in the forgiveness of God is that He forgets, the one thing a human being can never do. Forgetting is a Divine attribute; God's forgiveness forgets. God exhausts metaphors to show what His forgiveness means—"I, even I, am He that blotteth out thy transgressions for Mine own sake, and will not remember thy sins" (Isaiah 43:25); "I have blotted out, as a thick cloud, thy transgressions, and, as a cloud, thy sins" (Isaiah 44:22); "As far as the east is from the west, so far hath He removed our transgressions from us" (Psalm 103:12); "For I will forgive their iniquity, and I will remember their sin no more" (Jeremiah 31:34).ᴴˢᴳᴹ

Reflection Questions

Do I believe that God can deal with my "yesterday" and make it as though it had never been? What is the evidence?

FORGIVENESS IS THE miracle of grace. The great characteristic of God is not that He says He will pay no more attention to what we have done, but that He forgives us, and in forgiving He is able to deal with our past, with our present and our future.ᴴˢᴳᴹ

IT IS NOT a new gospel we need—that is the jargon of the hour. It is the old gospel put in terms that fit the present-day need. For one man or one book that does that there are hundreds who tell us that what we want is a new gospel. What we want is men who have the grace of their Lord to face the present-day problems with the old gospel. What is the good of my talking to the crowd of today about the conceptions men had in Luther's day? How does the gospel meet the problems they are facing? Can I show them where other solutions are wrong? If not, I had better keep quiet.ᵀᴴᴳ

Reflection Questions

Do I understand how God's grace works in today's world? Am I communicating it effectively? Do I believe that God's grace is sufficient at all times in all places?

WE HAVE TO guard against wanting to be somewhere else. Have I sufficient grace to behave as God's child where I am? It is one thing to feel the sufficiency of God in times of delight and excitement, but another thing to realize His sufficiency in settings that are difficult.ᵀᴴᴳ

Grace: God's Overflowing Favor

WHEN WE ARE born from above we are apt to despise the clay of which we are made. The natural creation and the creation of grace work together, and what we are apt to call the sordid things—laboring with our hands, and eating and drinking—have to be turned into spiritual exercises by obedience. Then we shall eat and drink, and "do all to the glory of God." Every power of mind and heart should go into the strenuousness of turning the natural into the spiritual by obeying the word of God regarding it. If we do not make the natural spiritual, it will become sordid; but when we become spiritual the natural is shot through with the glory of God.THG

Reflection Questions

Is the creation of grace making peace between my nature and my spirit so that my whole being brings glory to God? What is the evidence?

THE LORD CAN never make a saint out of a good man. He can only make a saint out of three classes of people—the godless man, the weak man, and the sinful man. The marvel of the Gospel of God's grace is that Jesus Christ can make us what He wants us to be.THG

A SINNER KNOWS what the Redemption has wrought in him, but it is only long afterward that he begins to grasp the revelation of how that Redemption was made possible in him. It is one thing to be saved by God's grace, but another thing to have a clear revelation as to how God did it. When the words of the Bible come home to us by the Holy Spirit, the supernatural essence of the Redemption is in those words and they bring forth new life in us. If you have been saved from sin, say so; if you have been sanctified by God's grace, say so. Don't substitute some other refinement in its place.ᵀᴴᴳ

Reflection Questions

In what ways do I minimize the work of grace in my life? What fancy words do I use that make a miracle sound like an academic exercise?

THE DANGER WITH those of us who have experienced God's perfect salvation is that we talk blatant jargon about an experience instead of banking on the tremendous revelation of God the Holy Ghost. The purer we are through God's sovereign grace, the more terribly poignant is our sense of sin.ᵀᴴᴳ

Grace: God's Overflowing Favor

THE CHARACTERISTIC OF being born again is that we know Who Jesus is. The secret of the Christian is that he knows the absolute Deity of the Lord Jesus Christ. When we are saved by God's grace our minds are opened by the incoming of the Holy Spirit and we understand the Scriptures. The test of regeneration is that the Bible instantly becomes the Book of books to us.[THG]

Reflection Questions

Do I see the Bible as an unfolding mystery of grace or as a confounding puzzle of truth? Am I a partner of the Author or a victim of the one who separates the Word from the Writer?

THE ONLY WAY to maintain perception is to keep in contact with God's purpose as well as with His Person. I have to place myself in relation to facts—facts in nature and facts in grace. If I refuse to do this my perception will be wrong, no matter how right my disposition may be; but the two together will produce a life perfectly in accordance with the life of the Son of God when He walked this earth.[THG]

GOD'S GRACE DOES not leave us after an experience of grace. The common idea of how to live the right life seems to be that it is by getting continual "bouts" of God's grace, that an insight into God's grace will last us several days. As a matter of fact it won't last us any time. That is not what God's grace means. When the work of God's grace begins, "the love of God is shed abroad in our hearts by the Holy Ghost," not the power to love God, but the essential nature of God. It is only by realizing the love of God in us by His grace that we are led by His entrancing power in us.ITWBP

Reflection Questions

What is the evidence that God's grace is working in me? Am I striving to be known or to make God known?

LOOKING UPON THE gifts of the Spirit as a favor to us is the first thing that will take us out of the central point of Jesus Christ's teaching. Never look at the work of God in and through you; never look at the way God uses you in His service. Gifts are gifts, not graces.ITWBP

Grace: God's Overflowing Favor

ONLY WHEN OUR lives are hid with Christ in God do we learn how to be silent unto God, not silent about Him, but silent with the strong restful certainty that all is well. What a lot of panicky sparrows we are. We chatter and tweet under God's eaves until we cannot hear His voice at all—until we learn the wonderful life and music of the Lord Jesus telling us that our heavenly Father is the God of the sparrows, and by the marvelous transformation of grace He can turn the sparrows into His nightingales that can sing through every night of sorrow. A sparrow cannot sing through a night of sorrow, and no soul can sing through a night of sorrow unless it has learned to be silent unto God—one look, one thought about my Father in heaven, and it is all right.ITWBP

Reflection Questions

Have I learned to be silent? Have I learned to be still and let the grace of God overflow?

TO DELIGHT IN sacrificing the natural to the spiritual means to be overflowing with the grace and love of God.ITWBP

BEWARE OF BEING carried off into any kind of spiritual ecstasy either in private or in public. When once God's mighty grace gets my heart wholly absorbed in Him, every other love of my life is safe; but if my love to God is not dominant, my love may prove to be lust. Nearly all the cruelty in the world springs from not understanding this. Lust in its highest and lowest form simply means I seek for a creature to give me what God alone can give, and I become cruel and vindictive and jealous and spiteful to the one from whom I demand what God alone can give.[ITWBP]

Reflection Questions

Have I learned to distinguish between love and lust? In what ways has grace kept me from being cruel and vindictive and jealous?

WHENEVER THE GRACE of God strikes a man's consciousness and he begins to realize what he is in God's sight, he becomes fanatical, if he is healthy. We have to make allowance in ourselves and others for "the swing of the pendulum," which makes us go to the opposite extreme of what we were before.[ITWBP]

Grace: *God's Overflowing Favor*

HAVE WE BEGUN to walk the practical path in grace? Do we know anything about the practice of pain? Watch what the Bible has to say about suffering, and you will find the great characteristic of the life of a child of God is the power to suffer, and through that suffering the natural is transformed into the spiritual. The thing we kick against most is the question of pain and suffering. We have naturally the idea that if we are happy and peaceful we are all right. Happiness is not a sign that we are right with God.ᴵᵀᵂᴮᴾ

Reflection Questions

Am I disappointed that grace doesn't keep me from experiencing pain and suffering? How has grace protected me in pain and suffering?

THE FIERY FURNACES are there by God's direct permission. It is misleading to imagine that we are developed in spite of our circumstances; we are developed because of them. It is mastery in circumstances that is needed, not mastery over them. We have to manifest the graces of the Spirit among things as they are, not to wait for the Millennium.ᴸᴳ

GOD'S SILENCES ARE His answers. If we only take as answers those that are visible to our senses, we are in a very elemental condition of grace. Has God trusted us with a silence, a silence that is absolutely big with meaning? That is His answer. The manifestation will come in a way beyond any possibility of comprehension. Are we mourning before God because we have not had an audible response? Mary Magdalene was weeping at the sepulchre—what was she asking for? The dead body of Jesus. Of Whom did she ask it? Of Jesus Himself, and she did not know Him! Did Jesus give her what she asked for? He gave her something infinitely grander than she had ever conceived—a risen Lord.[IYSA]

Reflection Questions

Am I willing to accept silence as an answer?
Do I spend more time mourning the loss of what was or awaiting the resurrection of what is to come?

O LORD, RISE in grandeur into our lives and ways and goings. Be a strong presence of healing and hope and grace and beauty this day.[KGD]

Grace: *God's Overflowing Favor*

LOOK BACK OVER your own history as revealed to you by grace, and you will see one central fact growing large—God is love. No matter how often your faith in such an announcement was clouded, no matter how the pain and suffering of the moment made you speak in a wrong mood, still this statement has borne its own evidence—God is love. When trial and difficulties await you, do not be fearful, whatever and whoever you may lose faith in, let not this faith slip from you—God is Love. Whisper it not only to your heart in its hour of darkness, but here in your corner of God's earth and man's great city, live in the belief of it; preach it by your sweetened, chastened, happy life; sing it in consecrated moments of peaceful joy, sing it to the world around you.[LG]

Reflection Questions
What is my song of grace?
Where and to whom am I singing it?

REMEMBER WHAT IT cost God to make His grace a free gift. It cost agony we cannot begin to understand. The historic Cross of Christ is the pinhole in actual history through which we view the purpose of God—Jesus Christ, "the Lamb slain from the foundation of the world."[BSUG]

DO NOT THINK only of what is yet to be; think of the invisible things which are here and now. Think of the weight of glory that may be yours by means of that difficult person you have to live with, by means of the circumstances you are in, the people you come in contact with day by day. The phrase "a means of grace" comes with a wonderfully new meaning when we think of it in this light.LG

Reflection Questions

In what ways am I being a means of grace rather than only a recipient? When opportunities to extend grace are presented in difficult circumstances do I resist or embrace them?

YOU HAVE BEEN asking the Lord to give you the graces of the Spirit and then some set of circumstances has come and given you a sharp twinge, and you say— "Well, I have asked God to bring out in me the graces of the Spirit, but every time the devil seems to get the better of me." What you are calling "the devil" is the very thing God is using to manifest the graces of the Spirit in you.LG

Grace: God's Overflowing Favor

PATIENCE IS THE result of well-centered strength; it takes the strength of Almighty God to keep a man patient. No one can remain under and endure what God puts a servant of His through unless he has the power of God. A happy heart and an unpaid salary; a high head and an empty pocket! That is the way it works out in reality, in perplexities such as sickness, the loss of friends, the inscrutable ways of God's providence. But through it all the grace of God comes. Draw now, not presently, on the grace of God. The one word in the spiritual vocabulary is NOW. Let circumstances bring you where they will, keep drawing on the grace of God.[LG]

Reflection Questions

What causes me to think that grace is limited and that I need to use it sparingly? What keeps me from being more generous with it?

ONE OF THE greatest proofs that you are drawing on the grace of God is that you can be humiliated without manifesting the slightest trace of anything but His grace in you.[LG]

BLAMELESSNESS IS NOT faultlessness; faultlessness was the condition of the Lord Jesus Christ. We never can be faultless in this life, we are in impaired human bodies; but by sanctification we can be blameless. Our disposition can be supernaturally altered until in the simplicity of life before God the whole limit is holy, and if that is to be done, it must be by the great grace of God.[LG]

Reflection Questions

In what ways do I take blamelessness for granted? Do I presume on God's grace by failing to consider what a miracle it is?

WE CAN NEVER be blameless by thinking about it, or by praying about it, but only by being sanctified, and that is God's absolute sovereign work of grace. It is not the perfection of attainment in thinking, or in bodily life, or in worship, but the perfection of a blameless disposition, nothing in it to censure, and that in the eyes of God who sees everything.[LG]

WINE COMES ONLY from crushed grapes, and the things Paul is mentioning here are the things which bring out the wine that God likes. You cannot be poured-out wine if you remain a whole grape; you cannot be broken bread if you remain whole grain. Grapes have to be crushed, and grain has to be ground; then the sweetness of the life comes out to the glory of God. Watch the circumstances of life; we get them fairly well mixed, and if we are getting more than enough of one kind, let us thank the Lord for it; it is producing the particular grace that God wants us to manifest.[LG]

Reflection Questions

In what ways have I been crushed? How is my life being poured out as a sweet offering?

FROM THE MOMENT that God uncovers a point of obstinacy in us and we refuse to let Him deal with it, we begin to be skeptical, to sneer and watch for defects in the lives of others. But when once we yield to Him entirely, He makes us blameless. It is not done by piety, it is wrought in us by the sovereign grace of God, and we have not the slightest desire to trust in ourselves in any degree, but in Him alone.[LG]

THE GRACE OF God never fails in a crisis; it is we who fail because we have not been practicing. To refuse to form mental habits is a crime against the way we are made. God has made us so that we can make our own mental habits, if we will. When we are regenerated God does not give us another body, we have the same body, and we have to get it working according to His teaching. Think of the time we waste in talking to God and in longing to be what He has already made us instead of doing what He has told us to do!ᴹᶠᴸ

Reflection Questions

What mental habits do I practice to prepare myself for crisis? How is God's character being formed in me? How am I an ally of grace?

THE MATTER OF behavior is ours, not God's. God does not make our character; character is formed by the reaction of our inner disposition to outer things. God does what we cannot do. Then begins our work, we must work out what God works in. The practicing is ours, not God's. We have to bring the body and brain into line and make it a strong ally of the grace of God.ᴹᶠᴸ

Grace: *God's Overflowing Favor*

BY HEEDING THE reality of God's grace within us we are never bothered again by the fact that we do not understand ourselves, or that other people do not understand us. If anyone understood me, he would be my god. The only Being Who understands me is the Being Who made me and Who redeems me, and He will never expound me to myself; He will only bring me into contact with Himself, and the heart is at leisure from itself for ever afterward.MFL

Reflection Questions

Why do I expect people to understand me when I can't even understand myself? What keeps me from simply celebrating the miracle that God knows and understands me?

BY GOD'S GRACE things have been done which are miraculous, so we become devoted to the miracle and forget God. Then when difficulties come we say it is the antagonism of the devil. The fact is we are grossly ignorant of the way God has made us. Stand up to the difficulty, and all that you ever believed about the transforming grace of God will be proved in your bodily life.MFL

IT IS THE natural instinct of a child to imitate his mother, and when we are born again the Holy Spirit lifts this instinct into the spiritual domain and it becomes the most supernaturally natural thing for us to imitate our Lord. We grow in grace naturally, not artificially. When you are good you never try to be. It is natural to be like the one we live with most; then if we spend most of our time with Jesus Christ, we shall begin to be like Him, by the way we are built naturally and by the Spirit God puts in us.[MFL]

Reflection Questions

Is it natural for me to be nice? Has the grace of the Lord become so much a part of me that kindness and generosity are my first response? In what ways do I fail to emulate Jesus?

OUR LORD BUILDS His deepest teaching on the instinct of emulation. Our example is not a good man, not even a good Christian man, but God Himself. By the grace of God I have to emulate my Father in heaven.[MFL]

Grace: God's Overflowing Favor

WHEN WE ARE born again we become natural for the first time; as long as we are in sin we are abnormal, because sin is not normal. When we are restored by the grace of God it becomes the most natural thing to be holy, we are not forcing ourselves to be unnatural. When we are rightly related to God all our natural instincts help us to obey Him and become the greatest ally of the Holy Spirit. We disobey whenever we become independent. Independence is not strength but unrealized weakness, and is the very essence of sin.MFL

Reflection Questions

Have I realized that dependence on God is natural, not supernatural? Have I considered that holiness is a condition God intended for us to enjoy, not grudgingly agree to?

IF I REFUSE to make my natural life spiritual by the slow process of obedience, my religious profession becomes a disgusting hypocrisy. Any attempt to build on the natural virtues will ultimately outrage the grace of God, whereas dependence on God means the successful working of God's grace in me.NE

IF SATAN CANNOT switch the saints off on false fire, he will switch them off on anything that is less than the central thing. The central thing is the life hid with Christ in God where we can stand by the grace of God, true to God and to God's aspect of things, letting other things shift as they may. "A man's life consisteth not in the abundance of the things which he possesseth" (Luke 12:15); it consists only in what he is. All our judgments of God, and our mis-judgments, are based on our own point of view, not on Jesus Christ's.[NI]

Reflection Questions

How much time do I spend on what makes me feel important? Why do I become frustrated when God doesn't cooperate?

THE NATURE OF faith is that it must be tested; and the trial of faith does not come in fits and starts, it goes on all the time. The one thing that keeps us right with God is the great work of His grace in our hearts. All the prophets had to take part in something they did not understand, and the Christian has to do the same. If we were to say "This is the way God is going to work," it would lead to spiritual pride.[NI]

Grace: God's Overflowing Favor

THE CHARACTERISTIC OF a child of God is that there is no deceit, nothing to hide from God (1 John 1:7). Never trust any man or woman, and never trust yourself, trust only the grace of God. As sure as we put our trust in man, no matter how good, we learn that the human heart is a cunning house of deceit. We all work for our own ends till we get into the light with God; then we have no end to serve, we are without guile. The only way to keep in the light is to remain true to Jesus Christ and not guard ourselves; let Him guard and let Him watch.ᴺᴶ

Reflection Questions

What do I trust that operates outside the grace of God? In what area do I struggle being honest?

WE MUST BE humorous enough to see the shallow tricks we all have, no matter what our profession of Christianity. The grace of God makes us honest with ourselves. We are so perverse that God had to come and save us! Whenever we forget this and begin to set up little standards of our own, we are sure to go wrong.ᴺᴺᵂ

JESUS CHRIST NOT only gives us ideals, but He shows us that men are incapable of attaining them, and He came that they might get there by the miracle of His grace. Other teachers never refer to the possibility of our getting there, and it is that kind of teacher we like. Men can never attain the ideal that God demands unless they attain it by regeneration through the cross of Christ; and that never comes in experience but by shame and repentance.[NJ]

Reflection Questions

In what way do I try to attain God's ideal apart from grace? Do I ever think of grace as a license to sin?

BEWARE OF EVER saying to yourself, "God's law is not exactly binding to me, I am under grace." To be under grace should mean that we can fulfil the law of God gracefully.[NJ]

Grace: God's Overflowing Favor

A CHRISTIAN KNOWS that the possibilities of every sin ever committed are in him but for the grace of God. The condemnation of sin before we are saved is bitter, intense, and proud. After we are saved, the sins of others come upon us with the twofold weight of the possibility of doing the like ourselves, and the possibility of vicarious intercession.[NJ]

Reflection Questions

How often do I thank God that His grace has kept me from reaching my full potential of depravity? What keeps me from being honest about the condition of my heart and mind?

THE ORDINARY OCCURRENCES of life reveal to us the condition of our hearts and minds. A dislike that will not forgive, is a natural condition that cannot be forgiven until a man wishes to turn from it. The great characteristic of the supernatural grace of God is put by Jesus on the line of forgiveness. Forgiveness is not an act, it is the supernatural manifestation of a miracle within us.[NJ]

THE WONDERFUL THING about real living experience is that it is never referred to as past, but merely as the entrance into what is now enjoyed. Beware of building your faith on your experience of God's grace instead of on God Who makes the experience possible.ᴺᴶ

Reflection Questions

Have I experienced real living or am I stuck in the doorway of grace trying to get through with everything I have accumulated? Have I been through the doorway of disgrace and failure or am I looking for a different entrance?

IT TAKES THE grace of God to go through disgrace unspoiled. If Jeremiah's distress makes you condemn him, pass it by; but if, according to the reason of this world, you understand that God's ways are foolishness, you will put Jeremiah's grief and staggered amazement within sight of Gethsemane and Calvary. Every problem is faced and fathomed in the prophecies of Jeremiah.ᴺᴶ

70

Grace: *God's Overflowing Favor*

TEMPORAL POWER IS merely the manifestation of a Divine purpose leaving ample room for the prostitution of that power. When once a man is placed in a position of honor under God's providence and does not maintain a right relationship to God, the very position in which God has put him will harden him away from God. Power we must have, whether we like it or not, but power is a terrible peril unless the life is rooted in God's grace.[NJ]

Reflection Questions

In what ways have I mishandled power? How does God's grace keep me from becoming hard-hearted and unyielding? What might happen if I had more patience with grace?

GOD'S PURPOSES ARE brought about not only by sovereign decrees but by the delightful acquiescence of His people. That is why it takes time. God does not badger us into His will. His will will be done, and the marvel of the grace of God is that the most eager longing we have is for His will.[NJ]

71

REJOICING BEFORE GOD that is not based on humility is not born of the Spirit of God; rejoicing is made possible by the Atonement only and is wrought by the Holy Spirit. Bit by bit God lets us see what the grace of God atones for. The only attitude a Christian can have is one of absolute humility. If we are anything at all in the holy life it is by the grace of God and no other way. The Apostle Paul never forgot what he had been. The deeper we go into the grace of God the more profound is our humility. There is no holiness without humility.ᴺᴶ

Reflection Questions

Has God's grace made me humble enough to be honest? What good can come of dishonesty?

WE TALK TOO much about heroism because the majority of us are only barely honest. There is only one heroic figure, the Lord Jesus Christ. We have to get out of the complacency of superiority that is apt to come when the grace of God has done anything for us; the most the grace of God succeeds in doing for us is to make us honest. There is only one holiness, the holiness of God, and unless that holiness is imparted to us by direct identification, we are not even honest.ᴺᴶ

Grace: God's Overflowing Favor

OUR LORD DID not pray that His disciples should be taken out of the world, but that they should be kept from the evil. It is nothing but unmitigated cowardice to get out of the world; we have to remain unspotted in the midst of it. If you cannot, the grace of God is a fiction. External surroundings make no difference to our inner life, but our inner life makes a telling difference on our surroundings. A sunbeam may shine into a hovel, but it can never be soiled. Let God engineer your circumstances where He likes, and you will be kept as the light.ᴺᴶ

Reflection Questions

What difference does grace make in me? What difference does grace in me make in my surroundings?

WHEN FACED WITH difficulties, we do not try to brace ourselves up by prayer to meet them, but by the power of the grace of God we let the perfections of Jesus Christ be manifested in us. Jesus Christ does not give us power to work up patience like His own. His patience is manifested if we will let His life dwell in us. In sanctification we do not draw from Jesus the power to be holy; we draw from Jesus the holiness that was manifested in Him.ᴼᴮᴴ

THE WAY TO believe is to listen first. "So then faith cometh by hearing, and hearing by the word of God." We are invited and commanded by God to believe that we can be made one with Jesus as He is one with God, so that His patience, His holiness, His purity, His gentleness, His prayerfulness are made ours. The way the gift of faith works in us and makes this real is by hearing. We first hear, and then we begin to trust. It is so simple that most of us miss the way. The way to have faith in the gospel of God's grace, in its deepest profundity as well as in its first working, is by listening to it.[OBH]

Reflection Questions

What voices do I listen to? What attitudes do I listen for? What do I hear that confirms the gospel of God's grace?

FAITH IS MORE than an attitude of the mind; faith is the complete, passionate, earnest trust of our whole nature in the Gospel of God's grace as it is presented in the Life and Death and Resurrection of our Lord Jesus Christ.[OBH]

WHAT DO WE do to earn a gift? Nothing; we take it. If we have the slightest remnant of thinking we can earn it, we will never take it; if we are quite certain we do not deserve it, we will take it. We come with the sense of abject unworthiness, knowing that "in me (that is, in my flesh,) dwelleth no good thing." If ever I am to be holy, I must be made holy by God's sovereign grace.[OBH]

Reflection Questions

Am I willing to accept the gift of grace or am I trying to make something of myself so that I will have something to give in exchange for it? Am I willing to be made new by God's grace or would I rather just redo the parts I don't like?

THE FULLEST AND most gracious meaning of regeneration and sanctification is that in Christ Jesus we can be made a new creation. Sanctification is not being given a new start, not that God wipes out the past and says it is forgiven, but something inconceivably grander, that is, that Jesus Christ has the power to create in us the image of God as it was in Himself.[OBH]

THE QUESTION OF forming habits on the basis of the grace of God is a very vital one. God regenerates us and puts us in contact with all His Divine resources, but He cannot make us walk according to His will; the practicing is ours, not God's. We have to take the initiative and "add to . . . faith virtue. . . ." To take the initiative means to make a beginning, and each one of us must do it for himself: We have to acquaint ourselves with the way we have to go, and beware of the tendency of asking the way when we know it perfectly well.[OBH]

Reflection Questions

Am I waiting for God to force me to conform?
What keeps me from accepting His offer
of transformation?

HAVE WE STOOD so long on the verge of a promise of God's that we have grown like monuments on its edge? If we were asked to go over the edge in the way of giving our testimony or doing something for God, would we feel awkward? It would be a good thing for us if we could be pushed over, no matter how we sprawled. If God tells us to do something good and we hesitate over obeying, we endanger our standing in grace.[OBH]

Grace: God's Overflowing Favor

IN ORDER TO express what God's grace has done in us we have to form habits until all habits are merged in the perfect relationship of love. God's commands are made to the life of His Son in us, not to our human nature; consequently all that God tells us to do is always humanly difficult; but it becomes divinely easy immediately we obey because our obedience has behind it all the omnipotent power of the grace of God. OBH

Reflection Questions

When disagreeable things happen, do I manifest the essential sweetness of the Son of God or the essential irritation of myself apart from Him? Which part of myself demands attention and keeps me from growing in grace?

WHENEVER SELF COMES into the ascendant, the life of the Son of God in us is perverted and twisted; there is irritation, and His life suffers. We have to beware of every element in human nature which clamours for attention first. Growth in grace stops the moment we get huffed. OBH

IN THE NATURAL world it is bad taste to talk about money; one of the worst of lies is tucked up in the phrase we so often hear—"I can't afford it." The same idea has crept into the spiritual domain; and we have the idea that it is a sign of modesty to say at the close of the day—"Well, I have got through, but it has been a severe tussle!" All the grace of God is ours through the Lord Jesus, and He is ready to tax the last grain of sand and the remotest star to bless us. What does it matter if circumstances are hard? Why shouldn't they be! We are the ones who ought to be able to stand them.[OBH]

Reflection Questions

In what ways do allow scarcity to affect my generosity? How do I insult God by behaving as if His grace is barely adequate?

THANK GOD IF you are going through a drying-up experience! And beware of pumping up the dregs with the mud at the bottom of the well when all the Almighty power and grace of God is at your disposal. We have super-abounding supplies, the unsearchable riches of Jesus Christ; and yet some of us talk as if our Heavenly Father had cut us off with a shilling![OBH]

Grace: God's Overflowing Favor

ARE YOU SULKING before God? Are the corners of your mouth, morally and spiritually, getting down and are you feeling sorry for yourself? You have turned your back upon God and are marching away from Him. Get straight to God, be abundantly stamped with His grace and His blessing will come through all the time; and when you get to heaven you will find that God has bound up the broken-hearted through you, has set at liberty the captives through you—but not if you have a murmur that "God is very hard." There is no self-pity left in the heart that has been bound up by the Lord Jesus Christ.OBH

Reflection Questions

How often do I feel sorry for myself when circumstances are hard? What keeps me from seeing the work that God's unlimited grace can accomplish?

WE OUGHT TO be going about like multimillionaires. We have all the grace of God to spend on others.OBH

THE GREATEST HINDRANCE of our spiritual life lies in looking for big things to do. Jesus Christ "took a towel. . . ." We are not meant to be illuminated versions; we are meant to be the common stuff of ordinary human life exhibiting the marvel of the grace of God. The snare in Christian life is in looking for the gilt-edged moments, the thrilling times; there are times when there is no illumination and no thrill, when God's angel is the routine of drudgery on the level of towels and washing feet. Routine is God's way of saving us between our times of inspiration.ᴼᴮᴴ

Reflection Questions

Am I content doing "little" things or am I always searching for something glamorous to make me feel important? When life sseems ordinary, what can I learn about God's extraordinary grace?

THERE IS SOMETHING in human pride that can stand big troubles, but we need the supernatural grace and power of God to stand by us in the little things.ᴼᴮᴴ

Grace: God's Overflowing Favor

GOD CREATED MAN to be His friend. When once the relationship of being the friends of Jesus is understood, we shall be called upon to exhibit to everyone we meet the love He has shown to us. Watch the kind of people God brings across your path, you will find it is His way of picturing to you the kind of person you have been to Him. The thing that keeps us going is to recognize the humor of our heavenly Father in it all, and we shall meet the disagreeable person with a spiritual chuckle because we know what God is doing. He is giving us a mirror that we may see what we have been like toward Him. Now we have the chance to prove ourselves His friends, and the other person will be amazed and will tumble into the grace of God.OBH

Reflection Questions

What kind of people does God bring into my life? What work of grace is God accomplishing in me through the people He brings to me?

GRACE IS THE overflowing immeasurable favor of God. The only thing that keeps back His grace and favor is our sin and perversity.OPG

Do you discern that Jesus Christ means His Atonement to be recognized there—in my home life, in my business? The grace of God is absolute, but your obedience must prove that you do not receive it in vain. Continually bring yourself to the bar of judgment and ask—Where is the discernment of the Atonement in this matter and in that? OBH

Reflection Questions

Where is the grace of God most needed in my life? Am I doing anything that would hinder its effectiveness? Am I willing to offer it to people who seem undeserving? What makes me think I have the right to decide?

The grace of God in a human being is proved by the discernment of the Atonement in unobtrusive practical ways. If the Atonement does not work out there, it will work out nowhere. Beware of the piety that denies the natural life, it is a fraud. We can all shine in the sun, but Jesus wants us to shine where it is dark. OBH

Grace: God's Overflowing Favor

AS LONG AS we live in a religious compartment, make our own theology, wear doctrinal "blinkers," and live only among those who agree with us, we shall not see where the shame comes in. But let God bring us into contact with those who are indifferent to what we believe, and we shall realize the truth of what our Lord said—"therefore the world hateth you." If we really believed our Lord's teaching it would make us a laughing stock in the eyes of the world. It requires the miracle of God's grace for us to believe what Jesus taught.OBH

Reflection Questions

Am I adequately prepared to withstand indifference and ridicule? Am I willing to associate with those who are hostile and angry? Am I strong enough to be gracious to them?

WHENEVER WE OBEY, the delight of the supernatural grace of God meets our obedience instantly. Absolute Deity is on our side when we obey, so that natural obedience and the grace of God coincide. Obedience means that we bank everything on the Atonement, and the supernatural grace of God is a delight.OBH

GOD NOT ONLY gives me supernatural grace, but He is in me to will and to do of His good pleasure. If I am a child of God, not only is God the source of my will, but God is in me to will. I do not bring an opposed will to God's will, God's will is my will, and my natural choices are along the line of His will. Then I begin to understand that God engineers circumstances for me to do His will in them, not for me to lie down under them and give way to self-pity. We are called to do God's will here and now. God not only expects me to do His will, but He is in me to do it.OBH

Reflection Questions

What circumstances has God engineered as an opportunity for me to do His will? How has He shown me that His grace is sufficient?

DOING GOD'S WILL is never hard. The only thing hard is not doing His will. All the forces of nature and of grace are at the back of the man who does God's will. We ought to be superabounding with joy and delight because God is working in us to will and to do His good pleasure. God's will is hard only when it comes up against our stubbornness.OBH

Grace: *God's Overflowing Favor*

THE NATURAL VIRTUES are not promises of what we are going to be, but remnants of what God created man to be. We have the idea that we can bank on our natural patience and truthfulness and conscientiousness. We can bank on nothing in heaven above or earth beneath but what the grace of God has wrought in us. Everything we possess in the way of moral property, of noble spiritual property, severs us from God; all must go. Immediately we abandon that, we experience what Paul says, "I have been crucified with Christ" (Galatians 2:20). The reconstruction of our lives proves that God has cleansed us from all dead works.[PS]

Reflection Questions
What has the grace of God shaped in me?
How is it making me one with God and
one with myself?

GOD'S PURPOSE IS to make us perfectly at one with all our own powers and perfectly at one with God, no longer children but understanding in our heads as well as in our hearts the meaning of the Redemption, and slowly maturing until we are a recommendation to the redeeming grace of our Lord Jesus Christ.[PS]

BE AS STERN and unflinching as God Almighty in your preaching, but as tender and gentle as a sinner saved by grace when you deal with a human soul. Jesus Christ taught His disciples never to keep back the truth of God for fear of persecution. But we have infinite pity and sympathy with other souls, keeping your eye on what you once were and what, by the grace of God, you are now.[PS]

Reflection Questions

In what ways does the grace of God make me more tender toward others who are not yet aware of God's offer of grace? What is the best way for me to communicate God's gospel of grace?

EVERYTHING DONE APART from God—all prayer, all preaching, all testifying, all kind, sacrificial deeds—are dead works that clog the life. Never forget that you are what you are by the grace of God. If you are not what you are by the grace of God, then may God have mercy on you! Everything we are that is not through the grace of God is dead. The curse of the saint is his goodness![PS]

JESUS CHRIST REPRESENTS the Bread of God broken to feed the world, and the saints are to be broken bread in His hands to satisfy Jesus Christ and His saints. When by the sanctifying power of the grace of God we have been made into bread, our lives are to be offered first of all to Jesus Christ. In the Old Testament the first fruits were always offered to God, and that is the symbol for our lives. The saint is meant to satisfy the heart of Jesus first, and then be used to feed His saints. The saints who satisfy the heart of Jesus make other saints strong and mature for God.SHL

Reflection Questions

Has grace become bread in my life? How do I distribute it? Who does it nourish?

THE GRACE OF God will make us marvelously impervious to tribulation and persecution and destitution because we are seated in heavenly places in Christ Jesus and cannot be awakened to self-pity. God sends His rough weather and His smooth weather, but we pay no attention to either because we are taken up only with one thing—the love of God in Christ Jesus.SHL

To USE THE word "economy" in connection with God is to belittle and misunderstand Him. Where is the economy of God in His sunsets and sunrises, in the grass and flowers and trees? God has made a superabounding number of things that are of no use to anyone. How many of us bother our heads about the sunrises and sunsets? Yet they go on just the same. Lavish extravagance to an extraordinary degree is the characteristic of God, never economy. Grace is the over-flowing favor of God. Imagine a man who is in love being economical![SHH]

Reflection Questions

Do I see God's grace in every sunrise?

Do I see His generosity in every sunset?

Do I see His extravagant goodness in science?

Do I see His lavish love in nature?

Do I see His glory in all creation?

OUR LORD MADE the way for every son of man to come into communion with God. The saints do not end in crucifixion; by the Lord's grace, they end in glory.[SSY]

Grace: God's Overflowing Favor

JESUS TOOK A fisherman and turned him into a shepherd. That is symbolic of what He does all the time. Indoor work has to do with civilization; we were created for outdoor work, both naturally and spiritually. The idea that we have to consecrate our gifts to God is a dangerous one. We cannot consecrate what is not ours (1 Corinthians 4:7). We have to consecrate ourselves, and leave our gifts alone. God does not ask us to do the thing that is easy to us naturally; He only asks us to do the thing we are perfectly fitted to do by grace.^{SSY}

Reflection Questions
What has God created me to do?
Where has He called me to do it?
Am I consecrated to the task?

WE ARE NOT here to serve our own purpose; we are here, by the grace of God and by His indwelling Spirit, to glorify our Lord and Master. If He brings us up against callous, mean, ungrateful, sponging people, we must never turn our faces for one second, because that is a temper of mind in which Jesus cannot be glorified.^{SSY}

IMAGINE A LILY hauling itself out of its pot and saying, "I don't think I look exactly right here." The lily's duty is to obey the law of its life where it is placed by the gardener. We are all inclined to say, "I should be all right if only I were somewhere else." There is only one way to develop spiritually, and that is by concentrating on God. Don't bother about whether you are growing in grace or whether you are being of use to others.ssm

---

Reflection Questions

Have I been waiting for the perfect place to grow in grace? Do I have the idea that it's impossible for God to perform a work of grace in my present circumstances? Do I use my situation as an excuse for my lack of grace?

JESUS CHRIST CAME to make the great laws of God incarnate in human life; that is the miracle of God's grace. We are to be written epistles, "known and read of all men." There is no allowance whatever in the New Testament for the man who says he is saved by grace but who does not produce the graceful goods.ssm

IT IS IMPOSSIBLE to enter into communion with God while in a critical temper. Criticism makes you hard and vindictive and cruel, and leaves you with the flattering unction that you are a superior person. It is impossible to develop the characteristics of a saint and maintain a critical attitude. The first thing the Holy Spirit does is to give us a spring-cleaning, and there is no possibility of pride being left in a man after that. I never met a man I could despair of after having discerned all that lies in me apart from the grace of God. Stop having a measuring rod for others. One of the severest lessons to learn is to leave the cases we do not understand to God. There is always one fact more in every life of which we know nothing, therefore Jesus says, "Judge not."[SSM]

Reflection Questions

Does my pride prevent God's grace from working in me? Does my critical attitude inhibit God's grace from working through me?

THE GREAT CHARACTERISTIC of the saint is humility. We realize to the full that all these sins and others would have been manifested in ourselves but for the grace of God. Therefore we have no right to judge.[SSM]

IF I HAVE let God remove the beam from my own outlook by His mighty grace, I will carry with me the implicit sunlight confidence that what God has done for me He can easily do for you, because you have only a splinter, I had a log of wood! This is the confidence God's salvation gives us. We are so amazed at the way God has altered us that we can despair of no one.[SSM]

Reflection Questions

Do I see clearly the work of grace in my life? Does grace continue to amaze me? Do I continually praise God for grace? Does the work of grace in my own life make me eager for others to experience it as well? Do I sow seeds of grace wherever I go?

EVERY GOOD THING we have has been given to us by the sheer sovereign grace of God. When you deal with others never forget that you are a sinner saved by grace. If you stand in the fullness of the blessing of God, you stand there by no other right than the sheer sovereign grace of God.[SSM]

Grace: God's Overflowing Favor

THE GOSPEL OF the grace of God takes the stain of memory from a worker, not by making him ignore the past, but by enabling him to see that God can make it of service in his work for God. A worker should never tell people to forget the past. If we forget the past we will be hard and obtuse. If we are hard, we are of no use to God; and unless we know the Cross of Christ as the power which takes the stinging stain out of memory and transforms it, we are of no use to others.[PH]

Reflection Questions

In what ways has grace redeemed my past? How has grace removed the stain and the sting of sin and hurt? How has grace softenend my heart and made me open to love?

THE HOLY SPIRIT will bring the worker back again and again to the stained places in memory and will make them the sweetest, the most radiant portion of that one's inner life with God. The great marvel of God's grace is that "where sin abounded, grace did much more abound."[PH]

MORAL AND SPIRITUAL integrity cannot be measured by God's blessings. God sends His favors on good and bad alike. The blessings of God are an indication that God is overflowing in grace and benediction regardless of a man's relationship to Him. Men may partake of the blessings of God and yet never come into relationship with Him. (See Matthew 5:45–48.)PH

Reflection Questions

How long did I enjoy God's grace before I acknowledged where it was coming from? What made me finally realize that all creation is an expression of God's grace? Why do I still have moments of thinking that I shouldn't enjoy it because I don't deserve it?

IT TAKES A long time to realize what Jesus is after, and the person you need most patience with is yourself. God takes deliberate time with us. He does not hurry, because we can only appreciate His point of view by a long discipline. The grace of God abides always the same. By His grace we stand on the basis of His Redemption.PH

Grace: God's Overflowing Favor

NO ONE ON earth is more mean than I am, no one more capable of doing wrong, and yet we are always more afraid of the other fellow than of ourselves. The forgiveness of God means that we are forgiven into a new relationship, that is, into identification with God in Christ, so that the forgiven man is the holy man. The only explanation of the forgiveness of God and of the unfathomable depth of His forgetting is the blood of Jesus. We trample the blood of the Son of God under foot if we think we are forgiven in any other way. Forgiveness is the Divine miracle of grace.[PH]

Reflection Questions

Do I minimize my own sinfulness? Do I exaggerate the sinfulness of others? Have I realized that forgiveness is not just a pardon for sin but the removal of guilt?

JESUS CHRIST NEVER trusted human nature, yet He was never cynical, never in despair about any man, because He trusted absolutely in what the grace of God could do in human nature.[PH]

IF WE COULD not disobey God, our obedience would not be worth anything. The sinless-perfection heresy says that when we are saved we cannot sin; that is a devil's lie. When we are saved by God's grace, God puts into us the possibility of not sinning, and our character from that moment is of value to God. Before we were saved we had not the power to obey, but now He has planted in us the heredity of the Son of God, we have the power to obey, and consequently the power to disobey. The walk of a disciple is gloriously difficult, but gloriously certain.ssm

Reflection Questions

If the grace of God gives me the power not to sin, why do I still want to sin? What remnant of desire has yet to be cleansed by God's grace?

WE HAVE NO right to call on God to do supernatural wonders. The temptation of the Church is to go into the "show business." When God is working the miracle of His grace in us it is always manifested in a chastened life, utterly restrained.ᴾᴴ

Grace: God's Overflowing Favor

WHEN WE BECOME rightly related to God, we are not simply put back into the relationship Adam was in, but into a relationship Adam was never in; we are put into the Body of Christ, and then God does not shield us from any of the requirements of sons. We have the notion at first that when we are saved and sanctified by God's supernatural grace, He does not require us to do anything, but it is only then that He begins to require anything of us.[PR]

Reflection Questions

How is living in Christ better than living in Eden? What does God require of me now that I have access to His Divine resources?

GOD REGENERATES US and puts us in contact with all His Divine resources, but He cannot make us walk according to His will. If we will obey the Spirit of God and practice through our physical life all that God has put in our hearts by His Spirit, then when the crisis comes we shall find that we have not only God's grace to stand by us but our own nature also, and the crisis is passed without any disaster, and exactly the opposite happens, the soul is built up into a stronger attitude toward God.[PR]

WE MUST ALWAYS distinguish between the truths we receive as revelations and what we experience of God's grace. We experience the wonderful reality of God's salvation and sanctification in our actual lives, but we also have to receive into our minds and souls Divine revelations which we cannot experience. We cannot experience Jesus Christ rising from the dead; we cannot experience His Destiny or His Deity, but we must understand where the regenerating forces in our lives come from. The New Testament insists on an instructed mind as well as a vital experience.[PR]

Reflection Questions

What revelation have I received by grace rather than by experience? How has grace changed my ignorance into understanding?

GOD GRANT US the grace to rely on the Holy Ghost, to know our ignorance, to get out of the way with our knowledge, that we will let the Holy Ghost bring the Majestic Christ face to face with the diseased, sick folk we meet.[WG]

Grace: *God's Overflowing Favor*

WHEN SOULS ARE born again into the kingdom of God the Church of Christ makes a tremendous rejoicing, as it ought to make, but then what does it do? When God brings souls to you who have been brought into His kingdom by His sovereign work of grace, what have you to do? Disciple them, and the only way you can disciple them is not by making them proselytes of your views, but by teaching them to do what Jesus commanded you to do and you have done.^{WG}

Reflection Questions

How has grace changed my attitude regarding obedience? How does grace keep me from creating duplicates of myself?

JESUS CHRIST'S LIFE must work through our flesh, and that is where we have to obey. So many go into raptures over God's supernatural salvation, over the wonderful fact that God saves us by His sovereign grace (and we cannot do that too much), but they forget that now He expects us to get ourselves to obey Him.^{PR}

IN THE BEGINNING of the life in grace we have to limit ourselves all round, in right things as well as wrong; but if when God begins to bring us out of the light of our convictions into the light of the Lord, we prefer to remain true to our convictions, we become spiritual lunatics. Walking in the light of convictions is a necessary stage, but there is a grander, purer, sterner light to walk in, which is the light of the Lord.[SSM]

Reflection Questions

Am I living in the light of my convictions or walking in the light of the Lord? Am I moving closer to the perfect balance of grace and truth?

ALWAYS ALLOW FOR the swing of the pendulum in yourself and in others. A pendulum does not swing evenly at first, it begins with a tremendous swing to one extreme and only gets back to the right balance gradually, and that is how the Holy Spirit brings the grace of God to bear upon our lives.[SSM]

Truth

God's Perfect Reality

IT IS HIS work in me He is counting worthy, not my work for Him. The truth is we have nothing to fear and nothing to overcome because He is all in all and we are more than conquerors through Him. He counts us worthy because He has done everything for us. It is a shameful thing for Christians to talk about "getting the victory." The overcoming referred to in the Book of the Revelation is not the personal overcoming of difficulties but the overcoming of the very life of God in us while we stand resolutely true to Him.[AUG]

Reflection Questions

Do I resist or assist the life of God in me? Do I give more time and attention to my work for God or His work in me? What is the truth about God and His work in the world?

WHAT IS NEEDED today is not a new gospel, but men and women who can re-state the Gospel of the Son of God in terms that will reach the very heart of our problems. We need men and women saturated with the truth of God who can re-state the old truth in terms that appeal to our day.[AUG]

Truth: *God's Perfect Reality*

BE KEEN IN sensing Scriptures that contain the truth which comes straight home, and apply them fearlessly. The tendency is to get a truth of God and gloss it over. God is more tender than anyone we can conceive of, and if a man cannot get through to Him it is because there is a secret thing he does not intend to give up. It is impossible to deal poetically with a case like that. You have to go right down to the root of the trouble. The Gospel of Jesus awakens a tremendous craving but also a tremendous resentment. People want the blessing of God, but they will not stand the probing and the humiliation.[AUG]

Reflection Questions

Am I honest with myself about who I am? Am I honest with God? In what ways do I try to change the truth by living in denial?

NEVER FORGET WHO you are, what you have been, and what you may be by the grace of God. When you try and re-state to yourself what you implicitly feel to be God's truth, you give God a chance to pass that truth on to someone else through you.[AUG]

CONCENTRATE ON THE deposit of truth conveyed by the words of Scripture. Never have as your ideal the desire to be an orator or a beautiful speaker; if you do, you will not be of the slightest use. An orator moves men to do what they are indifferent about; a preacher of the Gospel has to move men to do what they are dead-set against doing, that is, giving up the right to themselves.[AUG]

Reflection Questions

Whose truth do I more often preach, my own or God's? Whose point of view do I more often defend? Whose reputation do I more often protect?

CONCEIT MEANS MY own point of view and I don't care what anyone else says. Conceit makes the way God deals with me personally the binding standard for others. We are called to preach the Truth, Our Lord Jesus Christ, and we get decentralized from Him if we become specialists.[AUG]

Truth: *God's Perfect Reality*

INTENSITY OF COMMUNION is not in feelings or emotions or in special places, but in quiet, fixed, confident centering on God. Never allow anything to hinder you from being in the place where your spiritual life is maintained. The expression of our lips must correspond with our communion with God. It is easy to say good and true things without troubling to live up to them; consequently the Christian talker is more likely to be a hypocrite than any other kind of worker. In all probability you will find you could express things better a few months or years ago than you can now, because the Spirit of God has been making you realize since then what you are talking about, and through the consequent distress that laid hold of mind and heart you have been driven to find out the secret place of the Most High.^AUG

Reflection Questions

How often do I make time to center myself on God? Do I speak truth more than I live it?

THERE ARE CERTAIN points of truth Our Lord cannot reveal to us until our character is in a fit state to bear it. The discernment of God's truth and the development of character go together.^AUG

AM I LEARNING how to use my Bible? The way to become complete for the Master's service is to be well soaked in the Bible, some of us only exploit certain passages. Our Lord wants to give us continuous instruction out of His word; continuous instruction turns hearers into disciples. Beware of using the Bible for the sake of getting messages; use it to nourish your own soul. Be a continuous learner, don't stop short, and the truth will open to you on the right hand and on the left until you find there is no problem in human life with which the Bible does not deal.^AUG

Reflection Questions

Do I use the Bible to nourish my soul or to acquire information? Am I willing to accept truth even when it contradicts my feelings?

NEVER WATER DOWN or minimize the mighty Gospel of God by considering that people may be misled by certain statements. Present the Gospel in all its fullness and God will guard His own truth.^AUG

Truth: *God's Perfect Reality*

PERSONALITY SOMETIMES HINDERS the Gospel. People are swept off their feet not by the truth presented but by the tremendous force of the personality that presents it. Personality is used by God to emphasize a neglected truth, but the Toms, Dicks and Harrys are the ones used to spread a knowledge of salvation. That is the only standard for the preacher of the Gospel. We have no right as preachers on the ground of our personality, but only because of the message we proclaim.^{AUG}

Reflection Questions

In what situations have I been more influenced by a charismatic person than by biblical truth? How much do I rely on a person to tell me what to believe?

JESUS TOLD THE disciples that they would be opposed not only in private life, but that the powers of state would oppose them and they would have to suffer persecution, and some even crucifixion. If you stand true to Jesus Christ you will find that the world will react against you with a butt, not with a caress, annoyed and antagonistic (see John 15:18–20).^{AUG}

NEVER SYMPATHIZE WITH a soul who finds it difficult to get to God; God is never to blame. We have to present the truth so that the Spirit of God will show what is wrong. The element of judgment must always come out; it is the sign of God's love. The great sterling test in preaching is that it brings everyone to judgment; the Spirit of God locates each one. Never allow in yourself or in others the phrase "I can't"; it is unconscious blasphemy. If I put my inability as a barrier, I am telling God there is something He has not taken into account.^AUG

Reflection Questions

Which statement do I more often believe: "I can" or "I can't"? Why? What causes me to believe that God is limited by my weakness? What do I gain by saying "I can't"? False humility? False security?

PEOPLE WHO SAY "I can't" are those who have a remnant of self-reliance left. A true saint never says "I can't," because it never occurs to him that he can! Complete weakness is always the occasion of the Spirit of God manifesting His power.^AUG

Truth: *God's Perfect Reality*

THERE IS A difference between devotion to principles and devotion to a person. Hundreds of people today are devoting themselves to phases of truth, to causes. Jesus Christ never asks us to devote ourselves to a cause or a creed; He asks us to devote ourselves to Him, to sign away the right to ourselves and yield to Him absolutely, and take up that cross daily.^AUG

Reflection Questions

What cause do I place above Christ?

What doctrine do I believe instead of Christ?

What denomination do I trust more than Christ?

THE DANGER OF putting theology first is that it leads a man to tell a lie in order to be consistent with his point of view. Are we going to remain true to our religious convictions or to the God who lives behind them?—true to our denominational view of God or to the God who gave the denomination its initial inspiration? Are we going to be mere sticklers for the theological statement?^BFB

THE REASON JOB'S friends misunderstood was that they took Job's words and deliberately denied the meaning which they knew must be behind them, and that is a misunderstanding not to be easily excused. It is possible to convey a wrong impression by repeating the exact words of someone else, to convey a lie by speaking the truth.[BFB]

Reflection Questions

In what situations have I told the truth and perpetuated a lie? In what situations have I been told the truth by someone perpetrating a lie? What lies are more appealing to me than truth?

IF YOU TAKE an illustration from Nature and apply it to a man's moral life or spiritual life, you will not be true to facts because the natural law does not work in the spiritual world. What is true is that as there is a law in the natural world so there is a law in the spiritual world, that is, a way of explaining things, but the law is not the same in both worlds.[BFB]

Truth: *God's Perfect Reality*

GOD CAN NEVER be on the side of any individual; the question to ask is—"Am I on God's side?" Job says, "I am not going to say that my former definition of God is true; God must be true. but I find that the way I have expounded Him is not true." This put Job on the right track to find God. Are we on the trail of God, or on the obstinate, intolerant line, where we argue for our statements instead of for the truth? Does our religion put us on the line of understanding the revelation of God, or is it merely a blind authority? It is a good thing to take stock of the things which common-sense inferences and religion cannot explain.[BFB]

Reflection Questions

Do I argue more forcefully for my own interpretation of truth or for truth as God revealed it? In what way is my own interpretation a stumbling-block to others?

NO MAN EVER puts a stumbling-block in the way of others by telling the truth; to tell the truth is more honoring to God than to tell a lie. If God has done something for you, you will know it unmistakably, but if He has not, never say He has for the sake of other people.[BFB]

THE BASIS OF a man's faith in God is that God is the Source and Support of all existence, not that He is all existence. Job recognizes this, and maintains that in the end everything will be explained and made clear. Have I this kind of faith—not faith in a principle, but faith in God, that He is just and true and right? Many of us have no faith in God at all, but only faith in what He has done for us, and when these things are not apparent we lose our faith and say, "Why should this happen to me? I am going to chuck up my faith in God."[BFB]

Reflection Questions

What is the difference between having faith in God versus having faith only in what God does for me? How can I discern the difference between true and real?

TODAY MEN ARE not asking, "Is the thing true?" but "Is it real?" It is a matter of indifference whether a thing is true; any number of things can be demonstrated to be true which do not matter to us. Have I a real God, or am I trying to produce a Pharisaic cloak for myself?[BFB]

Truth: *God's Perfect Reality*

INTELLECT ASKS, "WHAT is truth?" as if truth were something that could be stated in words. "I am . . . the Truth," said Jesus. The only way we get at Truth is by life and personality. When a man is up against things it is no use for him to try and work it out logically, but let him obey, and instantly he will see his way through.[BFB]

Reflection Questions

Why do I think of truth as an idea that resides in my head? How should I think of it instead? Why is it so difficult to think of truth as a Person? What mistaken ideas do I have about Christ that pollute my perception of truth?

TRUTH IS MORAL, not intellectual. We perceive Truth by doing the right thing, not by thinking it out. Men have tried to get at the truth of Christianity head-first, which is like saying you must think how you will live before you are born. We instantly see the absurdity of that, and yet we expect to reason out the Christian life before we have been born into the realm of Jesus Christ.[BFB]

ANYTHING THAT CONTRADICTS the manifestation given in and through the Lord Jesus Christ cannot be true of God. Therefore we know that the character of God is noble and true and right, and any authority from God is based, not on autocracy or mere blind power, but on worthiness which everything in me recognizes as worthy, therefore I submit.[BFB]

Reflection Questions

In what ways is my faith flimsy? How is the true character of God being revealed in, through, and to me? What makes me afraid to think?

THE REASON MANY of us refuse to think and discover the basis of true religion is because evangelical Christianity has been stated in such a flimsy way. In refusing to stand by what was not true, Job uttered bigger things than he understood at the time. That is the way God uses men when they are rightly related to Him; He conveys His real presence as a sacrament through their commonplace lives.[BFB]

Truth: *God's Perfect Reality*

IF EVER WE are to see the domain where Jesus lives and enter into it, we must be born again, become re-generated by receiving the Holy Spirit; then we shall find that Truth is not in a creed or a logical statement, but in Life and Personality. Christianity does not consist in telling the truth, or walking in a conscientious way, or adhering to principles; Christianity is something other than all that, it is adhering in absolute surrender to a Person, the Lord Jesus Christ.[BFB]

Reflection Questions

Do I get more energized about speaking truth or living truth? What does that say about my view of truth? What lies do I tell about God by the way I live?

GOD IS NOT an abstract truth; He is the Eternal Reality, and is discerned only by means of a personal relationship. If I preach the right thing but do not live it, I am telling an untruth about God.[BFB]

THERE MAY BE conversions of heart which are not conversions of mind; the last thing a man comes to is the conversion of his mind. Our Lord refers to this instability in His parable of the sower and the seed—they receive the word gladly, but they have no root in themselves. They may have as many conversions as there are days in the year, and at the end of the year they remain the same unreliable emotional people, utterly incapable of resting in a stable point of truth, and they become eager adherents of every new interest. The main characteristic of young modern life today is an intense craving to be interested—literature, amusements, all indicate this tendency, and in religion the Church is apt to pander to the demand to be interested; consequently men won't face the rugged facts of the Gospel, because when the Holy Spirit comes in He challenges a man's will, demands a reconstruction of his whole life, and produces a change of mind which will work havoc in his former complacency.[BE]

Reflection Questions

What captivates me? Am I more interested in new ideas or eternal Truth?

Truth: *God's Perfect Reality*

THE INTRODUCTION OF anything into this world is cataclysmic: before a tree can grow it must be planted; before a human being can evolve he must be born—a distinct and emphatic crisis. Every child born into the world involves a cataclysm to someone, the mother has practically to go through death. The same thing is true spiritually. Being "born from above" is not a simple easy process; we cannot glide into the Kingdom of God. Common sense reasoning says we ought to be able to merge into the life of God, but according to the Bible, and in actual experience, that is not the order. What Jesus Christ came to do was to put human life on the basis of Redemption whereby any man can receive the heredity of the Son of God.[BE]

Reflection Questions

Why do I expect spiritual birth to be easy? Why do I expect spiritual growth to happen naturally? Why do I expect spiritual maturity to be effortless?

CHRISTIANITY IS NOT consistency to conscience or to convictions; Christianity is being true to Jesus Christ. Over and over again a man's personal relationship to Jesus Christ gets into his convictions and splits them, like new wine put into old wine-skins, and if he sticks to his convictions before long he will become anti-Christ. The standard for my conscience and for the conscience of the whole human race is the Cross, and if I do not take care to rectify my individual conscience by the Cross I end in criticizing God. The standard for the Christian is never—Is this thing right or wrong? but, is it related to the blood and passion and agony of the Cross of Christ?[BE]

Reflection Questions

Where do my convictions come from? Are they from Christ or from my own conscience?

THE CHRISTIAN REVELATION is that God is a personal Being and He is good. By "good," I mean morally good. Test all beliefs about God by that; do they reveal clearly that God is a good God, and that all that is moral and pure and true and upright comes from God?[BE]

Truth: God's Perfect Reality

THE SLIGHTEST DEFLECTION from the real truth about sin, and all the rest of the reasoning goes wrong. Once placed fundamentally right regarding the doctrine of sin, and the reasoning follows in good order. If you read carefully the modern statements regarding sin you will be amazed to find how often we are much more in sympathy with them than with the Bible statements. We have to face the problem that our hearts may be right with God while our heads have a startling affinity with a great deal that is antagonistic to the Bible teaching. What we need, and what we get if we go on with God, is an intellectual re-birth as well as a heart re-birth.[BE]

Reflection Questions

What is the basis for my belief? How can I determine if my beliefs are based on Christ or on my attempt to explain my own experiences?

HOW ARE WE to have a right heart relationship to God? By accepting His Spirit, and He will bring us where we can understand how God's grace works. If any man will receive the Spirit of God, he will find He will lead him into all truth.[BP]

THE BIBLE DOES not reveal all truth. We have to find out scientific truth and common-sense truth for ourselves, but knowledge of the Truth, our Lord Himself, is only possible through the reception of the Holy Spirit. "Howbeit when He, the Spirit of truth, is come, He will guide you into all truth." The Holy Spirit alone makes the Word of God understandable. The regenerating and sanctifying work of the Holy Spirit is to incorporate us into Christ until we are living witnesses to Him.[BE]

Reflection Questions

In what ways do I confuse scientific truth and spiritual truth? What kind of truth can I expect the Holy Spirit to teach me?

HELL IS THE place of angelic condemnation. It has nothing to do primarily with man. God's Book never says that hell was made for man, although it is true that it is the only place for the man who rejects God's salvation. Hell was the result of a distinct condemnation passed by God on celestial beings, and is as eternal as those celestial anarchists.[BP]

Truth: God's Perfect Reality

GOD DOES NOT contradict our social instincts, He alters them. Jesus said, "Leap for joy" when they shall "separate you from their company and cast out your name as evil, for the Son of man's sake," not for some crotchety notion or faddy idea of your own, or for some principle you have wedded yourself to, but, for My sake. When we are true to Jesus Christ, our sociability is lifted to a different sphere.[BP]

Reflection Questions

In what way has God altered my social instincts? How can I know if I am being rejected for Jesus' sake or for some false notion of my own?

OUR LORD NEVER teaches the annihilation of self; He reveals how self can be rightly centered, the true center being perfect love toward God (see 1 Corinthians 13:4–8). Until self is rightly related there, we either grovel or swell in greatness; both attitudes are untrue and need to be put right. The true center for self is Jesus Christ.[BP]

PERFECT LOVE TAKES no account of the evil done unto it. It was the reproaches that hit and scandalized the true center of His life that Jesus Christ noticed in pain. What was that true center? Absolute devotion to God the Father and to His will; and as surely as you get Christ-centered you will understand what the Apostle Paul meant when he talks about filling up "that which is lacking of the afflictions of Christ." Jesus Christ could not be touched on the line of self-pity. The practical emphasis here is that our service is not to be that of pity, but of personal, passionate love to God, and a longing to see many more brought to the center where God has brought us.BP

Reflection Questions

Why is it unwise to rely on my conscience?
How can I know if my life is centered
on Christ?

IT CAN NEVER be true to call conscience the voice of God. The difference in the records of conscience is accounted for by the varieties of traditional religions, etc. Whether a person is religious or not, conscience attaches itself to the highest he or she knows, and reasoning on that, the life is guided accordingly.BP

Truth: *God's Perfect Reality*

IF YOU ARE going to live for the service of your fellow-men, you will certainly be pierced through with many sorrows, for you will meet with more base ingratitude from your fellow-men than you would from a dog. You will meet with unkindness and "two-facedness," and if your motive is love for your fellow-men, you will be exhausted in the battle of life. But if the mainspring of your service is love for God, no ingratitude, no sin, no devil, no angel, can hinder you from serving your fellow-men, no matter how they treat you. You can love your neighbor as yourself, not from pity, but from the true centering of yourself in God.[BP]

Reflection Questions

Where does my love for others come from? Do I rely on my own willpower to love others or does it come from the life of Christ in me?

WHEN A MAN'S heart is right with God the mysterious utterances of the Bible are spirit and life to him. Spiritual truth is discernible only to a pure heart, not to a keen intellect. It is not a question of profundity of intellect, but of purity of heart.[BSUG]

THE APOSTLE PAUL does not say that Jesus thought nothing of Himself; He thought truthfully of Himself, He knew Who He was, but there was no self-assertion. That means Jesus never presumed on His equality with God, He did not continually assert it. There was only one brilliant moment in the life of Jesus, and that was on the Mount of Transfiguration. We do not know what the glory was which He had with the Father before the world was, but if we stand with Him on the Mount we see what He emptied Himself of.BSUG

Reflection Questions

How can I think truthfully about myself and others? What compels me to think of myself more highly or more lowly than others?

THE TYPE OF mind we are to form is that of true humility, the mind of Christ which He exhibited while on earth—utterly self-effaced and self-emptied—not the mind of Christ when He was in glory. If you are a saint, says Paul, manifest it by having the mind which was in Christ. One of the essential elements of Deity is the humility expressed in a baby and in Jesus Christ.BSUG

Truth: *God's Perfect Reality*

IF WE BASE our thinking on principles instead of on a Person we shall go wrong, no matter how devout or honest we are. The one great Truth to keep stedfastly before us is the Lord Jesus Christ; He is the Truth. Only the whole truth is The Truth, any part of the truth may become an error. If you have a ray of light on The Truth never call it the whole truth; follow it up and it will lead you to the central Truth, the Lord Jesus Christ.BSUG

Reflection Questions

What partial truth do I magnify? What partial truth do I minimize? Why am I "partial" to certain aspects of truth rather than others? How can I proclaim the whole truth?

IF WE PREACH the effects of Redemption in human life instead of the revelation regarding Jesus, the result in those who listen is not new birth, but refined spiritual culture, and the Spirit of God cannot witness to it because such preaching is in another domain. We have to see that we are in such living sympathy with God that as we proclaim His truth He can create in souls the things which He alone can do.COG

THE ETERNAL TRUTH is that God created me to be distinctly *not* Himself, but to realize Him in perfect love. If I allow that God teaches me to walk in His will, I shall allow my neighbor, whom I love as myself, the same certainty, although his way may seem so different. When other religions and philosophies and philologies sink inane and pass, Bible statements stand like eternal monuments, shrouded in ineffable glory: 'God is Light'; 'God is love'; 'God is holy.' Every attempted definition of God other than these sublime inspirations negates God, and we find ourselves possessed of our own ideas with never a glimpse of the living God.[CD]

Reflection Questions

What does it mean to be made in God's image? Why do I keep trying to make God in my image?

TO SEARCH FOR a word of God to suit one's case is never Divine guidance, but human caprice and inclination. The Holy Spirit brings to our remembrance what Jesus said and leads us into all truth to glorify Jesus Christ. In tribulation God brings Divine guidance by His Word.[CD]

Truth: _God's Perfect Reality_

GOD IS NOT an outward gush of sentiment nor a vague abstraction of impersonal good nature. God is a living, intense Reality. Until this truth is grasped, the puzzles and the questions are more than can be met. But when by the discipline of Divine guidance, we know Him, and He going with us gives us Rest, then Time and Eternity are merged and lost in that amazing vital relationship. The union is one not of mystic contemplation, but of intense perfection of activity, not the Rest of the placid peace of stagnation, but the Rest of perfect motion.[CD]

Reflection Questions

In what way are time and eternity lost when I rest in God? Why is it more restful to do God's work in His way rather than my way?

THE FIRST OBEDIENCE of Jesus was not to the needs of man but to the will of His Father. At the heart of every one of Our Lord's answers is this: "I came to do God's work in His way, not in My own way, though I am the Son of God."[BSUG]

TRUTH IS NOT a system, not a constitution, nor even a creed. Truth is the Lord Jesus Christ Himself, and He is the Truth about the Father just as He is the Way of the Father. We tend to make truth a logical statement— a principle instead of a Person. Profoundly speaking there are no Christian principles. But the saint, by abiding in Christ in the Way of the Fatherhood of God, discerns the Truth of God. Confusion arises when we try to live up to a standard merely constructed on His word.ᶜᴰ

Reflection Questions

How does abiding in Christ relieve the pressure of living up to principles listed in a creed?

THOSE WHO NAME the Name of Christ must realize that He is the Truth, not the proclaimer of it; that He is the Gospel, not the preacher of it; that He is the Way of the Fatherhood of God. What men and women need is the 'Fathering' of God, so that they may be held steady by the gentleness of God realized in Christ. Those who know it have a gracious ministry to maintain—by abiding in Him to reveal the truth as it is in Jesus in our going in and out among the devastated and distracted.ᶜᴰ

WRATH IS THE dark line in God's face, and is expressive of His hatred of sin. Civilization is the gloss over chaos and wrath. We are so sheltered that we are blinded to our need of God, and when calamity comes there is nothing to hold to. Over and over again in the history of the world man has made life into chaos. Men try to find their true life in everything but God, but they cannot.[CHI]

Reflection Questions

What examples have I seen of the chaos caused when I or others try to find truth apart from God? What excuses do I make for myself when I cause chaos? How is my response different when others cause chaos?

WHENEVER THE LASH of remorse comes, never try to prevent it, every bit of it is deserved. And if you are a worker, never tell a lie out of sympathy and say, "Oh well, you don't need to feel like that, you couldn't help it." Never tell a lie to another soul. The temptation is tremendously strong to sympathize with a man and prove a traitor to his soul's true instincts.[CHI]

WE DO NOT create truth, we receive it. The Giver is God, and every gift He offers is based on His knowledge of us; our attitude is to be that of receiving from Him all the time, and in this way we become sons and daughters of God. It requires the greatest effort, and produces the greatest humility, to receive anything from God; we would much sooner earn it. Receiving is the evidence of a disciple of the Lord; reasoning about it is the indication of a dictator to God.[CHI]

Reflection Questions

What gift have I received from God? What does it tell me about God's knowledge of me? Do I work harder at giving away the gift God gave me or helping others receive the gift God has for them?

WHAT WAS IT God condemned in the Cross? Self-realization. Have I come to a moral agreement with God about that? To say that what God condemned in the Cross was social sins is not true; what God condemns in the Cross is sin which is away further down than any moral quirks.[CHI]

Truth: *God's Perfect Reality*

AN ABIDING WAY of maintaining our relation to Reality is intercession. Intercession is striving earnestly to have my human soul moved by the attitude of my Lord. That is where our work lies, yet we shirk it by becoming active workers; we do things that can be tabulated and scheduled, and we won't do the one thing that has no snares. Intercession keeps the relationship to God completely open. Be careful not to enmesh yourself in more difficulties than God has engineered for you to know. If you know too much, more than God has engineered, you cannot pray, the condition of the people is so crushing that you can't get through to Reality. The true intercessor is the one who realizes that "we know not what we should pray for as we ought: but the Spirit [Himself] maketh intercession for us with groanings which cannot be uttered" (Romans 8:26).CHI

Reflection Questions

Do I insist on measurable results for all my work? Do I insist on knowing details or do I trust God to know what I need to pray?

THE CITADEL OF true religion is personal relationship to God, let come what will.CHI

THE TRUE CONCEPTION of Man is our Lord. Man got out of God's order, and we are brought back not merely into the original order, but into a much better position through our Lord, that is, we are to be "conformed to the image of His Son." We look at the things that are expressed externally; God looks at the tendency born in us. He knows, apart from all our pious phrases and pretences, whether we have been regenerated, He sees what the life will become.[CHI]

Reflection Questions

In what ways am I being conformed to the image of God? In what ways does God energize my spirit and accomplish His good pleasure in and through me?

MAN HAS KINSHIP with God as no other creation of God has; his true kinship is with God and nowhere else. When I receive the Holy Spirit He lifts my personality back into its primal relationship with God. Holy Spirit coming into my spirit never becomes my spirit; He energizes my spirit and enables me "to will and to do of His good pleasure."[CHI]

Truth: *God's Perfect Reality*

NO MAN BEGINS his Christian life by believing a creed.
The man with a dogmatic creed says, "You must believe
this and that." Jesus says, "Do the will," i.e., "commit
yourself to Me." Truth is not in a particular statement;
Truth is a person, "I am . . . the Truth." It is a mistake to
attempt to define what a man must believe before he
can be a Christian; his beliefs are the effect of his being
a Christian, not the cause of it. CHI

Reflection Questions

*Why is it impossible to have accurate beliefs
prior to conversion? What will keep me from
being swept off my feet by lies?*

IMMEDIATELY YOU LOSE sight of the central, majestic
figure of Jesus Christ you are swept off your feet by all
kinds of doctrine, and when big things hit you find your
religion does not stand you in good stead because your
creed does not agree with the Truth.CHI

NEVER PIN YOUR faith to a man's reputation as a servant of God, always watch for the Holy Spirit. If a man is talking the truth of God those who listen will meet it again whether they like it or not; if he is not talking God's truth they won't come across it any more. Whenever the grand simple sanity of the Holy Spirit's interpretation is wanting, hold the matter in abeyance. The one stamp of the right interpretation is its "warm" natural sanity, it is not fantastic or peculiar, it doesn't twist your brain, it makes you feel, "How marvelously simple and beautiful that is!"CHI

Reflection Questions

What is the danger of making truth too complicated? What is the danger of believing that I need to trust experts to explain truth?

WHEN YOU LISTEN to a preacher, how are you going to know whether he is teaching the truth of God? Only by spiritual intuition. You may know that God has wonderfully used a man in the past, but never make that your ground for heeding what he says now, for at any minute a man may be out of touch with God (cf. 1 Corinthians 9:27). CHI

Truth: _God's Perfect Reality_

A TEACHER IS simply meant to rouse us up to face the truths revealed in the Bible and witnessed to by the Holy Ghost. Watch the tendency which is in us all to try and safeguard God's truth. The remarkable thing is that God never safeguards His own truth; He leaves statements in this Book we can easily misrepresent, the only test is the Holy Spirit who leads us into all truth.[CHI]

Reflection Questions

What role do teachers play in my understanding of truth? How is truth repairing my conscience? Have I advanced to the details or am I still working on general principles?

ONLY AS WE obey the Spirit and keep in the light does the anointing abide. Our thinking and common-sense reasoning must be rigorously subordinated to the Spirit, and if we abide true to Him He repairs the damage sin has done to conscience and mind and keeps our thinking vital and true. Notice in your own life how He works. He begins with the big general principles and then slowly educates you down to the scruple.[CHI]

AFTER A TIME of rapt contemplation when your mind has been absorbing the truth of God, watch the kind of people God will bring round you—not people dressed in the garb of some saint, but ordinary commonplace people just like yourself. We imagine that God must engineer special circumstances for us, peculiar sufferings; He never does, because that would feed our pride; He engineers things which from the standpoint of human pride are a humiliation.CHI

Reflection Questions

What kind of people is God bringing into my life? What has He sent them to teach me? In what ways do my convictions need to be altered?

IT IS EASIER to be true to our convictions than to Jesus Christ, because if we are going to be true to Him our convictions will need to be altered. Once allow that Jesus Christ is all the New Testament proclaims Him to be, and you are borne on irresistibly to believe that what He says about Himself is true.DI

WHEN A MAN says he can't believe, don't argue with him on what he doesn't believe but ask him what he does believe, and proceed from that point; disbelief as often arises from temperament as from sin. Every man believes in a good character, then refer to Jesus Christ as the best character in history, and ask him to believe that what He says is likely to be true (e.g. Luke 11:13; John 3:16), and get him to transact business on that.[DI]

Reflection Questions

Do I insist that people believe "everything" at once or am I willing to build on the bit of truth they already believe? Am I willing to listen to what God has to say about my pet prejudices?

GOD DOES NOT thunder His truth into our ears, our attitude of mind must be submissive to revelation facts. Each one of us brings certain prejudices, civilized prejudgments, which greatly hinder our understanding of revelation facts.[DI]

137

THE EXISTENCE OF a truth is nothing to me until I am brought into the current of events where that particular truth is a living reality to me because it speaks the language of my conscious life. Reality must have its source outside me; my conscious experience is the sphere of Reality in me, but I must be careful never to confound the reality of my experience with Reality itself.ᴳᵂ

Reflection Questions

In what ways do I confuse the reality of my experiences with the Reality of truth? What revelation is God trying to help me understand in my present circumstances?

THE WHOLE OF the New Testament exposition in the inspiration of the Holy Spirit is in order that we might know where we have been placed by Almighty God's Redemption. Immediately we come in contact with Reality our thinking is based on revelation all the time, and as we maintain our relation to Reality we will find new revelations of truth flashing out continually from the word of God.ᴳᵂ

Truth: *God's Perfect Reality*

THE PERSONALITY OF Truth is the great revelation of Christianity—"I am . . . the Truth." Our Lord did not say He was "all truth" so that we could go to His statements as to a text-book and verify things; there are domains, such as science and art and history, which are distinctly man's domains and the boundaries of our knowledge must continually alter and be enlarged; God never encourages laziness. The question to be asked is not, "Does the Bible agree with the findings of modern science?" but, "Do the findings of modern science help us to a better understanding of the things revealed in the Bible?"GW

Reflection Questions

In what ways has science helped me to better understand God's revelation? How do science and Scripture work together to reveal God's plan for all creation?

AS "WORKERS TOGETHER" with God we are called upon not to be ignorant of the forces of the day in which we live. God does not alter, the truths of the Bible do not alter, but the problems we have to face do alter.DI

GOD GAVE HIS final revelation in Jesus Christ; then He set processes at work for the re-organization of the whole of humanity. Jesus Christ is the Truth, an Incarnate Ideal; to be "in Christ" means that through regeneration and sanctification that Ideal can become a reality, so that in my mortal flesh there is manifested that which is easily discerned to be "the life also of Jesus." We are to be incorporated into the truth. The ideal is not a vague end into which we evolve more or less blindly, we "grow up in all things into Him."GW

Reflection Questions

How and in what ways am I being incorporated into the life of Jesus? In what ways has the Spirit been guiding me into all truth?

"THE TRUTH" is our Lord Himself; "the whole truth" is the inspired Scripture interpreting the Truth to us; and "nothing but the truth" is the Holy Spirit, "the Spirit of truth," efficaciously regenerating and sanctifying us, and guiding us into "all the truth."GW

Truth: *God's Perfect Reality*

THERE IS A danger of seeing the truth clearly with our minds, while the life and character lag woefully behind. Who has not met with clearness in verbal doctrine, almost dictatorial clearness, and wrong, almost quite wrong, attitudes in life and conduct? Being "of the truth" refers to a condition of character. GW

Reflection Questions

Does my character match my convictions? Do my convictions match Christ? Do I make Christianity more difficult than Christ intended so that "common people" will not understand?

MUCH IS WRITTEN about our Lord speaking so simply that anyone could understand, and we forget that while it remains true that the common people heard Him gladly, no one, not even His own disciples, understood Him until after the Resurrection and the coming of the Holy Spirit, the reason being that a pure heart is the essential requirement for being "of the truth." "Blessed are the pure in heart: for they shall see God."GW

THE REALIZATION THAT my strength is always a hindrance to God's supply of life is a great eye-opener. A man who has genius is apt to rely on his genius rather than on God. A man who has money is apt to rely on money instead of God. So many of us trust in what we have got in the way of possessions instead of entirely in God. All these sources of strength are sources of double weakness. But when we realize that our true life is "hid with Christ in God," that we are "complete in Him," in whom "dwelleth all the fulness of the Godhead bodily," then His strength is radiantly manifested in our mortal flesh.[GW]

Reflection Questions

In what ways are my resources, strength, and knowledge a hindrance to God? Why do I think of such things as my "real" life? What is wrong with this thinking?

PEOPLE SAY THEY are tired of life; no man was ever tired of life; the truth is that we are tired of being half dead while we are alive. What we need is to be transfigured by the incoming of a great and new life.[GW]

Truth: *God's Perfect Reality*

OUR LORD NEVER made a fuss over anyone, and the reason He didn't could not have been that He was callous or indifferent, or that He was not tenderhearted, or that He did not understand every detail, but the fact remains that He did not make a fuss over anyone. He never pleaded, He never cajoled, He never entrapped; He simply spoke the sternest words mortal ears ever heard, and then let it alone. The rich young ruler was a clean, moral, fine, vigorous young man, with a desire for all that was noble and true, but he did not expect to hear what he did.GW

Reflection Questions

Why is the desire to know truth insufficient?

How did Jesus insert truth into conversations?

WHEN JESUS TALKED to the woman of Samaria He did not use a prescribed form of address. He told her Divine truth and made her aware of her sin. When He talked to the disciples on the road to Emmaus, their hearts burned within them. The characteristic of the man of God's method is that he can speak to a sinner and win him before the sinner knows where he is; he can speak to saints and make their hearts burn.GW

WHENEVER WE GO into work for God from any stand-point saving that of the dominance of God, we begin to patronize at once; unless we go as the bondservants of Jesus Christ we have no business to go at all. Jesus Christ became the towel-girt Servant of His own disciples. Never deal with people from the superior person's standpoint, God never blesses that; deal only by steadily presenting the Lord Jesus Christ. The characteristic of the holiness which is the outcome of the indwelling of God is a blazing truthfulness with regard to God's word, and an amazing tenderness in personal dealing.ᴳᵂ

Reflection Questions

What causes me to approach people from an attitude of superiority? What is the attitude of holiness? Do I regret sin or repent of it?

People are enchanted with the truth, sympathetic with the truth of God, but remaining in sin. "Repentance" is not in their vocabulary, only regret; there is no confession of sin, only admitting. Religion is turned into education, and the Christian life is made to mean a happy life instead of a new life.ᴳᵂ

Truth: *God's Perfect Reality*

MANY TODAY LIKE to hear the word of God spoken straightly and ruggedly. They are delighted with the stern truth about holiness, about the baptism of the Holy Ghost, and deliverance from sin. They take up a pose of religion, but they are not penitent; they change the truth God requires into a mere attitude. God not only requires us to have a right attitude but also to allow His truth to so react in us that we are actively related to Him. The real attitude of sin in the heart toward God is that of being without God; it is pride, the worship of myself, that is the great atheistic fact in human life.GW

Reflection Questions

Am I truly penitent or merely religious? Am I sympathetic to truth while remaining in sin?

HAVE WE FORGOTTEN about penitence? Has penitence ever rung down to our very soul, or have we only known regret? Have we ever known what it is to confess our sin, to unfold our life before God until there is nothing folded up, and God's penetrating truth has its way? If not, we shall find that it is perilously easy to have amazing sympathy with God's truth and remain in sin.GW

OVER AND OVER again we find sanctified people stagnate; they do not go back and they do not go on. They get stiller and stiller, and muddier and muddier—spiritually, not morally—until ultimately there comes a sort of scum over the spiritual life, and you wonder what is the matter with them. They are still true to God, still true to their testimony, but they have not exercised the God-given reason in them and got beyond the image of experiences and gone on to draw their life from God, which transcends all we call experience.ᴳᵂ

Reflection Questions

Where do I look for truth other than Jesus?
What happens when once I begin to think that I have learned all the truth I need to know?

WHEN ONCE YOU take any one of the great works of God as an end, or any one of the truths which depend on Jesus Christ, as the truth, you will go wrong, you are outside the guard of God. Allow nothing to take you away from Jesus Himself, and all other phases of truth will take their right place.ᴳᵂ

Truth: *God's Perfect Reality*

IT IS NOT true to say that God wants to teach us something in our trials. In every cloud He brings, God wants us to unlearn something. God's purpose in the cloud is to simplify our belief until our relationship to Him is exactly that of a child. God uses every cloud which comes in our physical life, in our moral or spiritual life, or in our circumstances, to bring us nearer to Him, until we come to the place where our Lord Jesus Christ lived, and we do not allow our hearts to be troubled.^{GW}

Reflection Questions

What does God want me to unlearn? What direction do I refuse to take? How long does it take before I admit that I am lost?

SO OFTEN WE are like a man crossing a moor who obstinately refuses to take any directions, and he goes on and on only to find himself hopelessly lost; then he humbly tracks back to the signpost and looking up, sees the way to go. God does not get angry with us, He simply waits until we realize that what He says is true.^{HSGM}

IF IN THE final issue the souls of those I have taught do not turn to Jesus when they see Him, I have been a traitor. In the New Testament it is never the personality of the preacher that counts, what counts is whether he knows how to direct those who come to him to Jesus. If a man preaches on the ground of his personality he is apt to be a detractor from Jesus. The only reason for presenting Jesus is that He is All-in-all to me absolutely. Many of us only know devotion to a creed, to a phase of evangelical truth, very few know anything about personal devotion to Jesus.[HSGM]

Reflection Questions

In what ways do I direct people to Jesus? Do I reserve "spiritual" work for church or is it a way of life that I practice wherever I am?

WE DISCERN SPIRITUAL truth not by intellectual curiosity or research, but by entreating the favor of the Lord, that is, by prayer and by no other way, not even by obedience, because obedience is apt to have an idea of merit.[HSGM]

RELIGION IS NEVER intellectual; it is always passionate and emotional. But the curious thing is that it is religion that leads to emotion, not emotion to religion. If religion does not make for passion and emotion, it is not the true kind. When you realize that you are saved, that God has forgiven your sins, given you the Holy Spirit, I defy you not to be carried away with emotion. Religion which makes for logic and reason is not religion, but to try to make religion out of emotion is to take a false step.[THG]

Reflection Questions

Is my walk of faith intellectual or emotional? Why do I emphasize one over the other? What makes me feel more safe in one environment than the other?

EMOTION IS NOT simply an overplus of feeling, it is life lived at white-heat, a state of wonder. To lose wonder is to lose the true element of religion. With God a thing is never too good to be true; it is too good not to be true.[THG]

ARE YOU RISING up early and sitting up late to try and unravel difficulties? You cannot do it. It is a great thing to get to the place where you countenance God and know He rules. It is not done by impulse but by a settled and abiding conviction based on God's truth and the discipline of life. I know that God rules; and He gives me power to perceive His rule. There is no use sitting up late or rising up early. I must do the work that lies before me, and avoid worry as I would the devil. If I take time from sleep, God's punishment rests on me; or if I take time in sleep when I should be working, He punishes me. Sloth is as bad as being a fussy workman in God's sight.THG

Reflection Questions

What does my schedule reveal about my belief about work? Do I see my work as being more important than God sees it? Am I more passionate about working for God or allowing Him to work through me?

IT IS NOT that we have to do work for God, we have to be so loyal to Jesus Christ that He does His work through us. We learn His truth by obeying it.HSGM

Truth: *God's Perfect Reality*

TRUTH IS OUR Lord Himself. Consequently any part of the truth may be a lie unless it leads to a relation to the Truth. Salvation, sanctification, the Second Coming are all parts of the Truth, but none is the Truth; and they are only parts of the Truth as they are absorbed by the Truth, our Lord Himself. We are not told to expound the way of salvation, or to teach sanctification, but to lift up Jesus, that is, to proclaim the truth.ITWBP

Reflection Questions

What lies do I tell by focusing on one aspect of truth? How is being true to Jesus different from being true to a doctrine about Him?

IN ANY WORK I do for God is my motive loyalty to Jesus, or do I have to stop and wonder where He comes in? If I work for God because I know it brings me the good opinion of those whose good opinion I wish to have, I am a Sadducee. The one great thing is to maintain a spiritual life which is absolutely true to Jesus Christ and to the faith of Jesus Christ.THG

GOD EXPECTS US to be intercessors, not dogmatic fault-finders. Locusts in their flight over a stream may drown by the million, but others keep coming until there is a way for the live ones to go over their bodies. God uses His saints in the same way. "The blood of the martyrs is the seed of the Church." There are prominent names in works of faith, but there are thousands of others whose names are not known. It is the same truth our Lord uttered regarding Himself, "Except a corn of wheat fall into the ground and die, it abideth alone: but if it die, it bringeth forth much fruit." The work to begin with may be a wondrous delight, then it seems to die out, and if you do not know the teaching of our Lord you will say it is dead; it is not, it has fallen into the ground and died in its old form, but by and by it will bring forth fruit which will alter the whole landscape.THG

Reflection Questions

Am I willing to accept the role God has assigned to me without being critical of those appointed to a different role?

IT IS PERILOUS to listen to the truth of God unless I open my will to it. THG

Truth: *God's Perfect Reality*

WHAT IS TRUE of Adam is true of every man and woman. This inheritance of covetousness is the very essence of the Fall, and no praying and no power of man, singly or banded together, can ever avail to touch it; the only thing that can touch it is the great Atonement of our Lord Jesus Christ. Let people think what they like about you, but be careful that the last thought they get is God. When we have gone from them, there must be no beauty or fascination in us that makes them long for us, the only remembrance left must be, "That woman was true to God"; "That man was true to God."[ITWBP]

*R*eflection *Q*uestions
What impression do I leave on people? Is it obvious to others that I am true to God?

THE **S**PIRIT OF God will never witness to testimonies that are not true to the Holy Ghost, not true to the nature of Jesus. If there is a dryness in our experience it is because we have begun to take the advice of someone other than God, have begun to try and make our experience like someone else said it should be.[ITWBP]

THERE IS NOT a saint among us who can give explicit reasonings concerning the hope that is in us, but we can always give this reason: we have received the Holy Spirit, and He has witnessed that the truths of Jesus are the truths for us. When we give that answer, anyone who hears it and refuses to try the same way of getting at the truth is condemned. If a man refuses one way of getting at the truth because he does not like that way, he ceases to be an honest man.*ITWBP*

Reflection Questions

In what ways does the Holy Spirit witness that the claims of Christ are true? What truth other than Jesus am I searching for?

THE WHOLE BASIS of modern Christian work is to evade concentration on God. We will work for Him any day rather than let Him work in us. When a man or woman realizes what God does work in them through Jesus Christ, they become almost lunatic with joy in the eyes of the world. It is this truth we are trying to state, that is, the realization of the wonderful salvation of God.*ITWBP*

Truth: *God's Perfect Reality*

THE TEACHER SENT from God clears the way to Jesus and keeps it clear. Souls forget about him because the vision of Jesus is the only abiding result. When people are attracted to Jesus Christ through you, see that you stay on God all the time, and their hearts and affections will never stop at you. Many a church has been crippled by the pastor or teacher who has won people to himself. The true man or woman of God makes you want to serve God all the more. Beware of stealing the hearts of the people. If you think, "It is my presentation of the truth that attracts," the only name for that is "thief," stealing the hearts of the sheep.ITWBP

Reflection Questions

What am I doing to clear the way for people to get to Jesus? What roadblocks do I set up?

"SHOW BUSINESS" IS creeping into the very ranks of the saved and sanctified—"We must get the crowds." We must not; we must keep true to the Cross; let folks come and go as they will, let movements come and go, let ourselves be swept along or not, the one main thing is—be true to the yoke of Christ, His Cross.ITWBP

SOME PRAYERS ARE followed by silence because they are wrong, others because they are bigger than we can understand. Did Mary and Martha get Lazarus back? They got infinitely more; they got to know the greatest truth mortal beings ever knew—that Jesus Christ is the Resurrection and the Life. It will be a wonderful moment for some of us when we stand before God and find that the prayers we clamored for in early days and imagined were never answered, have been answered in the most amazing way, and that God's silence has been the sign of the answer. Time is nothing to God. Prayers were offered years ago and God answered the soul with silence; now He is giving the manifestation of the answer in a revelation that we are scarcely able to comprehend.[IYSA]

Reflection Questions

Why do I expect God to have the same sense of urgency as I do? Why do I expect God to operate according to my timetable?

Truth: *God's Perfect Reality*

WHEN ONCE WE get calm before God and are willing to let Him do what He chooses, He gives us an outline of some of His massive truths. The majority of us have never allowed our minds to dwell as they should on these great massive truths; consequently sanctification has been made to mean a second dose of conversion. Sanctification can only be named in the presence of God, it is stamped by a likeness to Christ. When a little child wants to say something and has not a vocabulary, it speaks through gesticulations and facial workings, it has not the power of soul to express itself in words. A man has the Spirit of Jesus given to him, but he has not His mind until he forms it. We are to form the mind of Christ by letting His Spirit imbue our spirit, our thinking, our reasoning faculties, then we shall begin to reason as Jesus did, until slowly and surely the very Spirit that fed the life of Jesus will feed the life of our soul.[IYSA]

Reflection Questions

What prevents me from having the mind of Christ? What attitude do I have that cannot coincide with the life of Christ?

THE AVERAGE MAN is inarticulate about his belief, and the curious thing is he does not connect his belief in goodness and truth and justice with Jesus Christ and the churches because the churches have misrepresented Jesus Christ. We cannot "corner" God or spiritual life. To think we can is the curse of denominational belief.[LG]

Reflection Questions

How do churches misrepresent Christ? Do I put allegiance to my church or denomination above my devotion to Christ? Even though God is consistent in character why should I not expect Him to be consistent in behavior?

BEWARE OF MAKING God run in the mold of His own precedent, that means, because He did a certain thing once, He is sure to do it again, which is so much of a truth that it becomes an imperceptible error when we subtly leave God Himself out of it. We have taken ourselves so seriously that we cannot even see God, we are dictating to God.[IYSA]

Truth: *God's Perfect Reality*

TRUTH IS ALWAYS a vision that arises in the basis of the moral nature, never in the intellect. Immediately we are rightly related to God in moral relationships, instantly we perceive. We can always tell the difference between a man with a keen intellectual discernment and the man with moral discernment. The latter always appeals to the conscience, the former simply convinces the mind.[LG]

Reflection Questions

Am I more likely to be seen as having intellectual discernment or moral discernment? Which is more important? Am I willing to live by one central truth: that God is love?

WHEN WE ARE young we think things are simpler than they are; we have an idea for every domain. A man says he is a materialist, or an agnostic, or a Christian, meaning he has only one main idea, but very few will run that idea for all it is worth. Yet this is the only way to discover whether it will work, and the same thing is true in the idea of the Christian religion that God is Love.[LG]

GOD DID NOT create Adam to live on the mountain; He made him of the dust of the earth, that was his glory. Our Lord came down from the Mount into the valley and went on to the Cross where He was glorified; and we have to come down from the mount of exaltation into the drab life of the valley. It is in the sphere of humiliation that we find our true worth to God, and that is where our faithfulness has to be manifested.[LG]

Reflection Questions

What makes me think I belong on the mountain top of spiritual exhilaration? What keeps me from being content in the valley?

WE HAVE AN idea that we have to alter things, we have not; we have to remain true to God in the midst of things as they are, to allow things as they are to transmute us. "Things as they are" are the very means God uses to make us into the praise of His glory. We have to live on this sordid earth, among human beings who are exactly like ourselves, remembering that it is on this plane we have to work out the marvelous life God has put in us.[LG]

Truth: *God's Perfect Reality*

OUR LORD WAS never impatient with His disciples. He simply planted seed thoughts in their minds and surrounded them with the atmosphere of His own life. He did not attempt to convince them, but left mistakes to correct themselves, because He knew that eventually the truth would bear fruit in their lives. You cannot make a man see moral truth by persuading his intellect.LG

Reflection Questions

Am I content to plant seeds of the gospel or do I also try to make them sprout and grow? Am I as patient with others as Jesus is with me? Am I willing to wait for fruit?

THE WAY JESUS dealt with the disciples is the way He deals with us. He surrounds us with an atmosphere of His own life and puts in seed thoughts. He states His truth, and leaves it to come to fruition. The disciples did not understand what Jesus taught them in the days of His flesh; but His teaching took on new meaning when once they received the Holy Spirit.LG

THE ONLY WAY to prove spiritual truth is by experiment. We talk about justice and right and wrong. Are we prepared to act according to what we think? Are we prepared to act according to the justice and the right which we believe to be the character of God? If we are, we shall have no difficulty in deciding whether or not the teaching of Jesus Christ comes from God.[MFL]

Reflection Questions

Does my behavior match what I say I believe? Do I believe that justice is important to God? What do I do to uphold justice in my community? Am I more interested in being right than in being just?

YOU CAN NEVER argue anyone into the Kingdom of heaven. You cannot argue anyone any where. The only result of arguing is to prove to your own mind that you are right and the other fellow wrong. You cannot argue for truth; but immediately Incarnate Truth is presented, a want awakens in the soul which only God can meet.[MFL]

Truth: God's Perfect Reality

IF FOR ONE moment we have discerned the truth, we can never be the same again; we may ignore it, or forget it, but it will not forget us. Truth once discerned goes down into the subconscious mind, but it will jump up in a most awkward way when we least expect it. We may see no result in our congregation, but if we have presented the truth and anyone has seen it for one second, he can never be the same again. A new element has come into his life. It is essential to remember this and not to estimate the success of preaching by immediate results.MFL

Reflection Questions

Do I trust the effectiveness of truth or do I feel compelled to add things to it to make it more convincing? Do I understand that not all truth bears fruit at the same time?

A TRUTH MAY be of no use to us just now, but when the circumstances arise in which that truth is needed, the Holy Spirit will bring it back to our remembrance.MFL

THE THINGS OF truth are things which are in keeping with the Person of Truth, the Lord Jesus Christ: "I am . . . the Truth." Truth therefore means not only accuracy, but accuracy about something that corresponds with God. We must distinguish between an accurate fact and a truthful fact. The devil, sin, disease, spiritualism, are all accurate facts, but they are not truthful facts. The accuracy of facts and the accuracy of the facts of truth are two different things. Never say that things that are not of the truth are non-existent. There are many facts that are not of the truth, that is, they do not correspond with God. MFL

Reflection Questions

Why is it important to discern between accuracy and truthfulness? How can something be accurate but not truthful?

WE HAVE TO be true to God, not true only to our idea of God. NNW

Truth: *God's Perfect Reality*

THE WORD "HONEST" means something noble and massive, awe-inspiring and grand, that awakens our reverence and inspires sublime thoughts, as a cathedral does. The things of honesty make a man's character sublime, and Paul counsels us to think on these things. Anything that awakens the sense of the sublime is an honorable thing. In the natural realm a sunset, a sunrise, mountain scenery, music, or poetry will awaken a sense of the sublime. In the moral world, truthfulness in action will awaken it.^{MFL}

Reflection Questions

In what way do I sacrifice truthfulness about important matters by insisting on accuracy in minor matters?

TRUTHFULNESS IN ACTION is different from truthfulness in speech. Truth-speaking people are an annoyance, they spank children for having imagination; they are sticklers for exact accuracy of speech and would have everyone say the same thing, like gramophone records. They drag down the meaning of truth out of its sphere. So we mean truthfulness in action, a true act all through.^{MFL}

THINK OF THE times we have hindered the Spirit of God by trying to help others when only God could help them, because we have forgotten to discipline our own minds. It is the familiar truth that we have to be stern in proclaiming God's word, let it come out in all its rugged bluntness, unwatered down and unrefined; but when we deal with others we have to remember that we are sinners saved by grace. The tendency today is to do exactly the opposite, we make all kinds of excuses for God's word—"Oh God does not expect us to be perfect," and when we deal with people personally we are amazingly hard.MFL

Reflection Questions

In what situations do I use truth harshly? What do I expect to gain for myself or for God by proclaiming truth in an unkind way?

WE ARE NOT here to be specimens of what God can do, but to have our life so hid with Christ in God that those who see our good works will glorify our Father in heaven. There was no "show business" in the life of the Son of God, and there is to be no "show business" in the life of the saint.MFL

Truth: *God's Perfect Reality*

THE CALL OF God comes with a realization that what God says is true, but that does not prevent us from going through the trial of our faith in connection with actual details, and it is when we touch actual details that we begin to dispute with God and say, "But if I obeyed God here my sense of justice and right would be injured." To talk in that way means we do not believe God one atom, although we say we do. The knowledge of God's will is not in the nature of a mathematical problem. As we obey, we make out what is His will, it becomes as clear as daylight. We have to beware of giving credit to man's wisdom for the way he has taken, when all the time it is the perfect wisdom of God that is manifested through the simple obedience of the man. It is never the acute ability of the saint that is exhibited, but the astute wisdom of God.NNW

Reflection Questions

How is God's will for my life different from what I expected? How have I responded?

FANATICISM IS STICKING true to my interpretation of my destiny instead of waiting for God to make it clear.NNW

ABRAHAM WAS NOT a pledged devotee of his own convictions, or he would have slain his son and said the voice of the angel was the voice of the devil. There is always the point of giving up convictions and traditional beliefs. If I will remain true to God, He will lead me straight through the ordeal into the inner chamber of a better knowledge of God.NNW

Reflection Questions

In what ways do I resist when God changes my direction? What do I gain by resisting? What do I lose?

IT IS EASIER to be true to convictions formed in a vivid religious experience than to be true to Jesus Christ, because if we are true to Jesus Christ our convictions have to be altered. Unless our experiences lead us on to a life, they will turn us into fossils; we will become mummified convictions. Error lies in making the basis of truth an abstraction, or a principle, instead of a personal relationship. Reality is not found in logic; Reality is a Person.NNW

Truth: *God's Perfect Reality*

GOD WILL NEVER have us follow Him blindly, He won't amaze us, He won't dazzle us with sudden floods of light. He breaks His revelation bit by bit as we will accept it. The appeal made by Jesus Christ is His character, His truth and His beauty, every man's conscience when he sees Him says, "That Man is right." There is nothing of the nature of the superstitious. The supernatural power of Satan never reasons, it appeals to man's superstition, not to his conscience.[NI]

Reflection Questions

Am I satisfied with God's revelation of His character or am I disappointed that He doesn't set forth a detailed multi-year plan for my life? How does the misinterpretation of truth lead to bitterness and cynicism?

BITTERNESS AND CYNICISM are born of broken gods; bitterness is an indication that somewhere in my life I have belittled the true God and made a god of human perfection.[NNW]

THE TERRIBLE SIDE of God's character is only realized by us when the truth dawns on us individually that God is no respecter of persons. Beware of tying God up in His own laws and saying He can't do what He says He is going to do. The greatest ingredient in the sovereignty of God is the measure of free will He has given man; but be careful you don't make the sovereignty of God the binding of Almighty God by human logic.[NE]

Reflection Questions

In what way do I try to bind God with the limitations of my understanding? In what ways does my shallowness keep me from a proper fear of God?

WE ARE TOO shallow to be afraid of God. All the Hebrew prophets reveal this truth, that there is only one Cause and no "second causes." It requires a miracle of grace before we believe this. Consequently we are foolishly fearless, but when the grace of God lifts us into the life of God we fear nothing and no one saving God alone.[NE]

Truth: God's Perfect Reality

THE GREAT TRUTH which runs all through God's Book
and takes clearer features in the New Testament is that
the material universe and the moral universe are from
the same Hand. Man was intended by God to govern
Nature (see Genesis 1:26). Instead, he has infected it
with his sin and it has become a partaker of the curse
with him, so that "the whole creation groaneth and tra-
vaileth in pain together until now."[NI]

Reflection Questions
How does immorality affect the material world?
How does my sin affect nature?

WE HAVE NO standing before God physically, morally
or spiritually; the only way we can ever stand before
God is through the Atonement. It is truths like this that
enable us to understand the meaning of the Cross. Sin
has infected the material universe as well as human nature, and both must be cleansed and purged. If I can
see how it works in my individual life I will see how it
works in the world at large.[NI]

THE TEST OF true religion is the knowledge of the character of God. As long as you think of God in the quietness of a religious meeting you will never know God. God's Book reveals that it is in the midst of what is opposite of God that His blessings occur. The very things which seem to be making for destruction become the revealers of God. It is an easy business to preach peace when you are in health and have everything you want, but the Bible preaches peace when things are in a howling tumult of passion and sin and iniquity. It is in the midst of anguish and terror that we realize who God is and the marvel of what He can do.[NI]

Reflection Questions

In what ways has God's grace prepared me for times of trouble? What have I found out about God during tumult that I could not have learned any other way?

THE DANGER WITH us is that we do not stand in the thick of things as the prophets did. We stand aloof and are no use in the way God intends us to be. Whatever the circumstances, we have to stand true for God there.[NI]

Truth: *God's Perfect Reality*

WE ARE APT to think that any one who has faced death and has seen the true issues of life will never become small and mean again, but that is a great fallacy. When we forget to walk in the light of the vision the meanness and selfishness will crop up again. Hezekiah forgot the grand stately processional gait and he degenerated into a childish piece of disgraceful conduct (see Isaiah 39). If you have had a spiritual awakening, a time of the sense of God's presence and revelation of His word, a crisis you can only account for by God, remember: The crisis in which God was revealed is to be the light of your life when there is no crisis.[NI]

Reflection Questions

What happens when I stray from the path of truth? Why does it take a crisis to make me realize I am lost? How can I get back into the light?

IN A CRISIS leave everything to God, shut out every voice saving the voice of God and the psalm of your own deliverance. Make it your duty to remain true to both these voices.[NI]

THERE ARE WHOLE tracts of God's character unrevealed to us as yet, and we have to bow in patience until God is able to reveal the things which look so dark. The danger is lest we make the little bit of truth we do know a pinnacle on which we set ourselves to judge everyone else. It is perilously easy to make our conception of God like molten lead and pour it into our specially designed mold and then when it is cold and hard, fling it at the heads of the religious people who don't agree with us. The stamp of the saint is not the metallic rapping out of a testimony to salvation and sanctification, but the true humility which shows the fierce purity of God in ordinary human flesh.[NI]

Reflection Questions

Is my faith as tender as the heart of Jesus or as hard as an iron idol? Do I place more confidence in things that are as solid as stone or as flexible as living water?

MEASURE YOUR ULTIMATE delight in God's truth and joy in God by the little bit that is clear to you. [NI]

Truth: God's Perfect Reality

THE FALSE PROPHETS comforted the people in their vain belief. Such prophets speak from themselves, and the emptiness of their prophecies falls upon their own heads. God's omnipotence will not enforce moral truth upon an unwilling mind; there must be an open mind and heart before the truth of God can be received. A prejudiced mind can only see along the line of its prejudices. Beware of saying, "I will never be in that state of mind." Any state of mind possible to any human being is possible in every human being.[NJ]

Reflection Questions

What are my prejudices? How do they affect my speech, my behavior, my witness, my worship?

LIFE IS TRAGIC, and we must get out of our glib notions. We drift into the line of good taste and civilized preaching and a winsome personality, and when we come to the truth of the Cross of Christ, we are in a totally other world, and if the world revealed in the Bible is a true world, most of us live in a fool's paradise. The views expressed in the Bible are always intense, but never exaggerated.[NJ]

Stealing, murder, immorality may never be performed physically, but a vestige of thinking along that line, Jesus says, is as bad in God's sight. Human nature hates God's message that there is a bad tendency inside that has to be plucked out, and unless it is it will damn us. It is extraordinary that although this truth is insisted on all through the Bible from Genesis to Revelation, it is the one thing we do not believe.[NJ]

Reflection Questions

What wickedness do I see in others that I cannot see in myself? Why do I get so emotional about the infractions of others and remain stoic about my own?

Paul emphasizes the fact that God is a sovereign Being, not a sentimental blessing. The Bible instills iron into our nature, it leaves none of the weak, sentimental things we hold in such esteem. The Bible is packed full of the most stern truths, yet it is anything but pessimistic. The Hebrew Scriptures know nothing about overwhelming sadness, they are optimistic.[NJ]

Truth: God's Perfect Reality

WE MUST REMAIN true to the revelation we have had, otherwise the condemnation will come on us that came on the false prophets of old. We are here for one purpose—to stand for the revelation of God's truth to the people of God and to sinners. The tendency is to water down God's truth in the case of some darling relationship and say God did not mean what we know He did. We must never shield a person from God's truth. If we do, we put them into the dark and deepen their torture instead of their peace.ᴺᴶ

Reflection Questions

What truth so enamors me that I am unwilling to move toward deeper revelation? What dark space has God called me to make brighter with His truth?

THE TRUTH ABOUT God is Jesus Christ—light, life, and love. Whatever is dark to us will, by means of our obedience, become as clear as the truth which we have made ours by obedience. The bit we do know is the most glorious, unfathomable delight conceivable, and that is going to be true about everything to do with God and us. The process is continual obedience.ᴺᴶ

IF YOU STAND for God's truth you are sure to experience reproach, and if once you open your mouth to vindicate yourself, you lose everything you were on the point of gaining. Let the ignominy and shame come. When Paul said, "I can do all things through Christ which strengtheneth me," they were weak things he spoke about—how to be abased, to be hungry, to suffer need. That is the test of a Christian, the power to descend until you are looked upon as absolute refuse and you have not a word to say any more than your Lord had. Only in that condition see that your faith in God does not fail.NJ

Reflection Questions

What is my understanding of "the power to descend"? Where have I seen God's blessing turn into a curse because it was used inappropriately?

THE TRUTH OF the moment is brought by Jesus into relation with Himself, the Truth. He will not allow us to rest in any detail of truth. Unless it is rooted in Him, it will turn to a curse instead of blessing.NJ

Truth: _God's Perfect Reality_

THE PRESENTATION OF the Gospel of God to sinners is one of love and mercy, but to the house of God one of judgment and truth. When we preach to the crowd outside we lambaste drunkenness and other things. Jesus never did. The stern messages of the Bible are never given to sinners, but to God's people.[NJ]

Reflection Questions

Do I proclaim love and mercy or judgment and truth to people who don't yet know Jesus? Why can I not rely on my own logic? Why am I still surprised to discover that Christianity is counter-intuitive?

GOD DOES NOT act according to His own precedents. Therefore logic or a vivid past experience can never take the place of personal faith in a personal God. It is easier to be true to a conviction formed in a vivid religious experience and say, "I will never alter that," than to be true to Christ, because if I am true to Christ, my convictions will have to be altered.[NJ]

WE CAN ONLY detect the express speaking of the Spirit by the same Spirit being in us. We do not naturally rely on the Spirit of God to expound God's word, we use our own intelligence. We think of God as being "somewhere," and we think of the hereafter in terms of space and time. When the Spirit of God expounds the spiritual life He does not deal with locations. "Am I a God at hand, saith the Lord, and not a God afar off?" There is neither "near" nor "far" with God. We have to un-learn our parochial notions about God, that is, the idea that He is interested in our local circumstances; the truth is that God enables us to be interested in Him in our local circumstances.ᴺᴶ

Reflection Questions

Why do I assume that I immediately know what work God wants me to do? Why do I resist any form of waiting to find out?

THE GREAT CRAZE today is work: God's word is "wait." Patience means standing under and enduring until the strain is past. The Spirit of God never adopts the tactics of the world. Remain uncrushably true to Jesus Christ wherever the providential order of God places you.ᴺᴶ

Truth: God's Perfect Reality

BEWARE OF BEING misled by affinities for certain aspects of God's truth, which makes us liable to be deluded. Every movement of the Spirit of God springs from the same source, and the counterfeit is to try and make the effect of one revival the cause of another. To exploit God's word by curiosity instead of relying on the Spirit of God is ever misleading. Obedience is the only line of illumination. If you pry into truths before God has engineered the circumstances in which those truths can be obeyed, you will go wrong. A clever exposition is never right, because the Spirit of God is not clever (cf. Matthew 11:25).[NJ]

Reflection Questions

What questions am I trying to answer on the basis of my experience? How might the answers be different if I started with obedience?

THINGS ARE DARK and obscure to us because we are not in a right condition to understand them. Thank God for all that we have understood, for every bit of truth that is so full of light and liberty and wonder that it fills us with joy.[OBH]

GOD CREATED THE world and everything that was made through the Son. Therefore just as God created the world through Him, the Son is able to create His own image in anyone and everyone. Have we ever thought of Jesus as the marvelous Being Who can create in us His own image? "Wherefore if any man is in Christ, there is a new creation"! (2 Corinthians 5:17). We do not sufficiently realize the wonder of it. Those of us who are in the experience of God's mighty salvation do not give ourselves half enough prayerful time, and wondering time, and studying time to allow the Spirit of God to bring this marvelous truth home to us.ᴼᴮᴴ

Reflection Questions

What does it means to be made in the image of God and re-made in the image of Christ? How much time am I willing to devote to find out?

TO UNDERSTAND THE tiniest bit of truth about God is to love it with all our heart and soul and mind. All that lies dark and obscure now will one day be as radiantly and joyously clear as the bit we have seen. No wonder God counsels us to be patient. ᴼᴮᴴ

Truth: *God's Perfect Reality*

JUST AS I take food into my body and assimilate it, says Jesus, so I must take Him into my soul. "He that eateth Me, even he shall live by Me." Food is not health, and truth is not holiness. Food has to be assimilated by a properly organized system before the result is health, and truth must be assimilated by the child of God before it can be manifested as holiness. We may be looking at the right doctrines and yet not assimilating the truths which the doctrines reveal. Beware of making a doctrinal statement of truth the truth—"I am . . . the Truth," said Jesus. Doctrinal statement is our expression of that vital connection with Him. If we divorce what Jesus says from Himself, it leads to secret self-indulgence.OBH

Reflection Questions

What truths have I ingested but not yet digested? How does this make me spiritually obese?

WE HAVE TO assimilate truth until it becomes part of us, and then begin to manifest the individual characteristics of the children of God. The life of God shows itself in different manifestations, but the aim ultimately is the manifestation of Jesus Christ.OBH

WHAT SATAN TOLD Eve is true, death does not strike them all at once: but its possibility has come in. Death has secretly begun. We transgress a law of God and expect an experience akin to death, but exactly the opposite happens—we feel enlarged, more broad-minded, more tolerant of evil, but we are more power-less. Knowledge which comes from eating of the tree of the knowledge of good and evil, instead of instigating to action, paralyzes.OPG

Reflection Questions

In what ways have I been deceived—both before sinning and after? Why are lies more appealing than truth? Why is it more thrilling to use my free will to do evil than to do good?

THE DISCIPLE WHO is in the condition of abiding in Jesus is the will of God, and his apparent free choices are God's foreordained decrees. Mysterious? Logically absurd? But a glorious truth to a saint.OBH

Truth: *God's Perfect Reality*

WE ARE ALWAYS inclined to remain true to our own ideas of a person. It does not matter what the facts are, we interpret all that he does according to our idea of him. If I accept you as an expression of my idea of you, I will be unjust to you as a fact. I make you either better or worse than you are, I never hit just "you" until I learn to accept facts as facts. The way I will discern God's character is determined by my own character. God remains true to His character, and as I grow in integrity I discern Him.OPG

Reflection Questions

In what situations do I pick and choose facts to support what I want to believe rather than to lead me to truth? Why do I prefer my own opinions over real truth?

IF I TELL a lie in order to bring about the right, I prove to my own conviction that I do not believe the One at the back of the universe is truthful. Judge everything in the light of Jesus Christ, who is The Truth, and you will never do the wrong thing however right it looks.OPG

I HAVE NEVER known a man or woman who taught God's word to be always acceptable to other people. Truths are all the time coming into your own life which you would never have seen for yourself, and as you give other people truths they never saw before, they will say—"I don't agree with that." It is foolish to begin to argue, if it is God's truth leave it alone; let mistakes correct themselves.[PS]

Reflection Questions

How do I handle disagreement? Do I argue for my point of view or allow truth the time to prove itself? Am I being united with God in true spiritual rest or would I rather rest in spiritual blessings?

THE DESIRE AT the heart of true spiritual life is for union with God. The tendency to rest in anything less than the realization of this desire becomes the arrest of desire. Whenever we seek repose in any blessing spiritually, sleeping sickness begins. The tendency to rest in any of the blessings which are the natural outcome of union with God is the beginning of backsliding.[PS]

Truth: *God's Perfect Reality*

ONE OF THE saddest things to see is men and women who have had visions of truth but have failed to apprehend them, and it is on this line that judgment comes. It is not a question of intellectual discernment or of knowing how to present the vision to others, but of seeking to apprehend the vision so that it may apprehend us. Soak and soak and soak continually in the one great truth of which you have had a vision; take it to bed with you, sleep with it, rise up in the morning with it, continually bring your imagination into captivity to it, and slowly and surely as the months and years go by God will make you one of His specialists in that particular truth.PS

Reflection Questions

What vision has God given to me? What have I done with it? What will I do with it?

What am I afraid of?

IT IS EASIER to stand true to a testimony which is moldy with age because it has the dogmatic ring about it that people agree with, than to talk from your last moment of contact with God.RTR

THE EYE IN the body records exactly what it looks at. The eye simply records, and the record is according to the light thrown on what it looks at. Our Lord Jesus Christ is the only true light on God. When a man sees Jesus Christ he does not get a new conscience, but a totally new light is thrown upon God, and conscience records accordingly, with the result that he is absolutely upset by conviction of sin.[PS]

Reflection Questions

How do I see God differently in the light of the Lord Jesus? How do I see people differently? How do I see circumstances differently? How do I see my sin differently?

THE SPIRIT OF God brings us to face ourselves steadily in the light of God until sin is seen in its true nature. If you want to know what sin is, don't ask the convicted sinner, ask the saint, the one who has been awakened to the holiness of God through the Atonement. He is the one who can begin to tell you what sin is.[PS]

Truth: *God's Perfect Reality*

JESUS CHRIST TAUGHT His disciples never to keep back the truth of God for fear of persecution. When we come to dealing with our fellow-men, what is our attitude to be? Remember yourself, remember who you are, and that if you have attained to anything in the way of holiness, remember Who made you what you are. "But by the grace of God I am what I am," says the Apostle Paul (1 Corinthians 15:10). Deal with infinite pity and sympathy with other souls, keeping your eye on what you once were and what, by the grace of God, you are now.[ps]

Reflection Questions

What is my attitude toward others? How often do I form opinions even though I have no knowledge of their circumstances?

GOD'S BOOK REVEALS all through that holiness will bring persecution from those who are not holy. Our Lord taught His disciples never to hide the truth for fear of wolfish men (Matthew 10:16). Personal experience bears out the truth that a testimony to holiness produces either rage or ridicule on the part of those who are not holy.[ps]

MODERN TEACHING IMPLIES that we must be grossly experienced before we are of any use in the world. That is not true. Jesus Christ knew good and evil by the life which was in Him, and God intended that man's knowledge of evil should come in the same way as to our Lord. That is, through the rigorous integrity of obedience to God. When a man is convicted of sin he knows how terrific is the havoc sin has wrought in him and he knows with what a mighty salvation he has been visited by God. But it is only by obedience to the Holy Spirit that he begins to know what an awful thing sin is.SHL

Reflection Questions

In what ways have I experienced evil? In what circumstances have I been deceived into thinking that evil was good? In what situations have I witnessed sin destroy beauty?

THE PRESENTATION OF true Christian experience brings us face to face with spiritual beauty; a beauty which can never be forced or imitated, because it is a manifestation from within of a simple relationship to God that is being worked out all the time.SHL

190

Truth: *God's Perfect Reality*

ONE OF THE most cunning travesties of Satan is to let us believe that he is the instigator of drunkenness and external sins. Man himself is responsible for doing wrong things, and he does wrong things because of the wrong disposition that is in him. The true blame for sin lies in the wrong disposition, and the cunning of our nature makes us blame Satan when we should blame ourselves.[SHL]

Reflection Questions

How often do I blame Satan for my own bad behavior? Why am I so reluctant to accept blame for my own bad choices?

DON'T PREACH OUT of natural discretion, but out of spiritual discretion which comes from intimacy with God. The prophet is more powerful than the priest or king. Jesus never spoke with the sagacity of a human being, but with the discretion of God. Beware of saying what is expedient from your own common-sense standpoint, especially when it comes to the big truths of God.[SHL]

GOD'S SEED WILL always bring forth fruit if it is put in the right conditions. Man cannot order the seasons or make the seed to grow (cf. Jeremiah 33:20). As preachers and teachers we are powerless to make saints. All we can do is to sow the seed of the Word of God in the hearts of hearers. The words our Lord uttered in reference to Himself are true of every seed: "Except a corn of wheat fall into the ground and die, it abideth alone; but if it die, it bringeth forth much fruit."SHL

Reflection Questions

What work do I try to do that belongs to God?
What work do I not do that He assigned to me?

MODERN EVANGELISM MAKES the mistake of thinking that a worker must plow his field, sow the seed, and reap the harvest in half-an-hour. Our Lord was never in a hurry with the disciples, He kept on sowing the seed whether they understood Him or not. He spoke the truth and by His own life produced the right atmosphere for it to grow. Then He left it alone. He knew that the seed had in it all the germinating power of God and would bring forth fruit.SHL

Truth: *God's Perfect Reality*

SOLOMON SAYS THAT God's judgment is right and true and that a man can rest his heart there. It is a great thing to notice the things we cannot answer just now, and to waive our judgment about them. Because you cannot explain a thing, don't say there is nothing in it. There are dark and mysterious and perplexing things in life, but the prevailing authority at the back of all is a righteous authority, and a man does not need to be unduly concerned.SHH

Reflection Questions

What makes me think that God needs my help to implement His judgments? Why do I expect a different standard of justice for myself than for others?

ONE OF THE great stirring truths of the Bible is that the man who looks for justice from others is a fool. Never waste your time looking for justice; if you do you will soon put yourself in bandages and give way to self-pity. Our business is to see that no one suffers from our injustice.SHH

WHEN A MAN is in a right relationship to God ritual is an assistance—the place of worship and the atmosphere are both conducive to worship. We are apt to ignore that ritual is essential in a full-orbed religious life, that there is a rectitude in true worship brought about only by the right use of ritual. For instance, when Jesus Christ taught His disciples to pray, He gave them a form of prayer which He knew would be repeated through the Christian centuries.SHH

Reflection Questions

In what ways does ritual enhance my worship? In what ways does it inhibit my worship? In what ways do I criticize the rituals of others while remaining ignorant of my own?

THERE MAY BE times when ritual is a good thing and other times when it is not. Bear in mind that in the Hebrew religion there is an insistence on ecclesiasticism and ritual. In the New Testament that is finished with (see John 4:21–24); but Ezekiel prophesies that the true worship of God will yet be established on earth as it has never yet been, and there will be ritual then to an extraordinary degree.SHH

Truth: *God's Perfect Reality*

DON'T BE FANATICALLY religious and don't be irreverently blatant. Remember that the two extremes have to be held in the right balance. If your religion does not make you a better man, it is a rotten religion. The test of true religion is when it touches these four things—food, money, sex, and mother earth. These things are the test of a right sane life with God, and the religion that ignores them or abuses them is not right.SHH

Reflection Questions

What is the difference between being completely devoted and fanatically religious? Which am I? In what ways has my faith made me a better person?

THE ESSENTIAL ELEMENT in moral life is obedience and submission. If you want spiritual truth, obey the highest standard you know. One ounce of chastity is worth fifty years of intellect in moral discernment. Moral truth is never reached by intellect. When a fine keen intellect and moral obedience go together, we find the mind that is beginning to discover step by step where goodness and truth lie.SHH

GOD'S JOB IS to alter my heredity. I cannot do it. But I have to manifest my altered heredity in actual circumstances. This is true in every domain. For instance, God won't clear up our social conditions; Jesus Christ is not a social Reformer. He came to alter us first, and if there is any social reform done on earth, we will have to do it. We are not to ask God to do what He has created us to do, any more than we are to attempt to do what He alone can do. Prayer is often a temptation to bank on a miracle of God instead of on a moral issue—it is much easier to ask God to do my work than it is to do it myself. Until we are disciplined properly, we will always be inclined to bank on God's miracles and refuse to do the moral thing ourselves.^{SA}

Reflection Questions

In what ways has God changed me and equipped me for the work He called me to do? In what domain has God assigned me to work?

IF WE REMAIN true to Jesus Christ we will encounter hostility when we come in contact with the culture and wisdom and education that is not devoted to Jesus.^{SSY}

Truth: *God's Perfect Reality*

MOST OF US have no ear for anything but ourselves. We are dead to, and without interest in the finest music. We can yawn in a picture gallery and be uninspired by a sunrise or a sunset. That is true not only of the soul's denseness to natural beauties, or to music and art and literature, but true with regard to the awakening of the soul to the call of God. To be brought within the zone of God's voice is to be profoundly altered.^{SSY}

Reflection Questions

If I am unmoved by art and beauty, how can I appreciate the creativity of God? If I remain unmoved by the creative ability that God gives to others, how will God be able to use me in recreating the beauty of His world?

JESUS APPEARS IN the most illogical connections, where we least expect Him, and the only way a worker can keep true to God amid the difficulties of work either in this country or in heathen lands is to be ready for His surprise visits. We have not to depend on the prayers of other people, not to look for the sympathy of God's children, but to be ready for the Lord.^{SSY}

WORSHIP IS THE love offering of our keen sense of the worth-ship of God. True worship springs from the same source as the missionary himself. To worship God truly is to become a missionary, because our worship is a testimony to Him. It is presenting back to God the best He has given to us, publicly not privately. Every act of worship is a public testimony, and is at once the most personally sacred and the most public act that God demands of His faithful ones.^{SSY}

Reflection Questions

What does my worship tell the world about my relationship with God? How does my worship exhibit the disposition of Jesus?

A TRUE WITNESS is one who lets his light shine in works that exhibit the disposition of Jesus.^{SSY}

Truth: *God's Perfect Reality*

IT IS POSSIBLE to say truthful things in a truthful manner and to tell a lie in thinking. I can repeat to another what I heard you say, word for word, every detail scientifically accurate, and yet convey a lie in saying it, because the temper of my mind is different from the temper of your mind when you said it. A lie is not an inexactitude of speech, a lie is in the motive. I may be actually truthful and an incarnate liar. It is not the literal words that count but their influence on others.SSM

Reflection Questions

Under what circumstances do I speak true details while trying to convey a false impression? How often do I intend to deceive even when I am speaking factually?

THE TEST JESUS gives is not the truth of our manner but the temper of our mind. Many of us are wonderfully truthful in manner but our temper of mind is rotten in God's sight. The thing Jesus alters is the temper of mind.SSM

THE KIND IMPUDENCE of the average truth-teller is inspired of the devil when it comes to pointing out the defects of others. We are all shrewd in pointing out the mote in our brother's eye. It puts us in a superior position, we are finer spiritual characters than they. Where do we find that characteristic? In the Lord Jesus? Never! The Holy Ghost works through the saints unbeknown to them. He works through them as light.[SSM]

Reflection Questions

Am I as eager to tell the truth about myself as I am to reveal it about others? How often has being criticized made me a better person? Why do I expect criticism to help anyone else?

A MAN WHO is continually criticized becomes good for nothing, the effect of criticism knocks all the gumption and power out of him. Criticism is deadly in its effect because it divides a man's powers and prevents his being a force for anything. That is never the work of the Holy Ghost. The Holy Ghost alone is in the true position of a critic; He is able to show what is wrong without wounding and hurting.[SSM]

Truth: *God's Perfect Reality*

THE CENTRAL TRUTH is not Salvation, nor Sanctification, nor the Second Coming. The central truth is nothing less than Jesus Christ Himself. Error always comes when we take something Jesus Christ does and preach it as the truth. It is part of the truth, but if we take it to be the whole truth we become advocates of an idea instead of a Person, the Lord Himself. If we are true only to a doctrine of Christianity instead of to Jesus Christ, we drive home our ideas with sledge-hammer blows. When we follow Jesus Christ, the domineering attitude and the dictatorial attitude go and concentration on Jesus comes in.ˢˢᴹ

Reflection Questions

What is my favorite spiritual tool? A hammer for pounding truth or a flashlight for revealing it?

HUMILITY AND HOLINESS always go together. Whenever hardness and harshness begin to creep into the personal attitude toward another, we may be certain we are swerving from the light. The preaching must be as stern and true as God's word. Never water down God's truth; but when you deal with others never forget that you are a sinner saved by grace.ˢˢᴹ

IF HUMAN LOVE is always discreet and calculating, never carried beyond itself, it is not of the true nature of love. The characteristic of love is that it is spontaneous, it bursts up in extraordinary ways; it is never premeditated. The reason Jesus called Mary's act "a good work" was because it was wrought out of spontaneous love to Himself. It was neither useful nor her duty; it was an extravagant act for which no one else saw any occasion. The very nature of God is extravagance. How many sunrises and sunsets does God make?PH

Reflection Questions
Is my worship discreet and calculating or spontaneous and exhuberant? Am I stingy or extravagant in expressing my love for God? What reason does Jesus have for calling my work "good"?

THE TRUE NATURE of devotion to Jesus Christ must be extravagance.SHH

Truth: God's Perfect Reality

THE CIRCUMSTANCES OF our Lord were anything but ideal. They were full of difficulties. Perhaps ours are the same. If so, we have to watch that we remain true to the life of the Son of God in us, not true to our own aims and ends. There is always a danger of mistaking our own aim and end for the aim of the life of God in us. Consider the subject of the call of God. The call of God is a call according to the nature of God; where we go in obedience to that call depends on the providential circumstances God engineers. The danger is to fit the call of God into the idea of our own discernment and say, "God called me there." If we say so and stick to it, then it is good-bye to the development of the life of God in us. We have deliberately shifted the ground of His call to fit our own conception of what He wants.[PR]

Reflection Questions

Am I being true to Jesus or to my own objectives? Have I been called to a place or to a Person?

TRUTH IS NOT discerned intellectually, it is discerned spiritually.[PR]

Index of Selections

Note to the Reader

The publisher invites you to share your response to the message of this book by writing Discovery House Publishers, P.O. Box 3566, Grand Rapids, MI 49501, U.S.A. For information about other Discovery House books, music, videos, or DVDs, contact us at the same address or call 1-800-653-8333. Find us on the Internet at www.dhp.org or send e-mail to books@dhp.org.